WHEN WAR IS UNJUST

WHEN WAR IS UNJUST

Being Honest in Just-War Thinking

Second Edition

————————◆————————

JOHN HOWARD YODER

Wipf & Stock
PUBLISHERS
Eugene, Oregon

Wipf and Stock Publishers
199 W 8th Ave, Suite 3
Eugene, OR 97401

When War is Unjust
Being Honest in Just-War Thinking
By Yoder, John Howard
Copyright©1996 Yoder, Anne Marie
ISBN: 1-57910-781-8
Publication date 10/10/2001
Previously published by Orbis Books, 1996

Dedicated to those courageous persons,
from the Vietnam War to the Persian Gulf,
who refused to serve in a war they considered unjust,
despite the fact that their understanding
of the just-war tradition had received little support
from their churches, schools, and families,
and even though their country's laws
refused to honor that conscientious stance.

Contents

Preface

Ecumenical encounter is defined by the recognition that if we differ from fellow-believers in our concrete decisions about action, we probably differ too in the kinds of logical and historical paths whereby we got to these contradictory conclusions.

Respectful dialogue therefore demands the exercise of entering into one's interlocutor's stance and story in search of some common court of appeal before which the clashing claims of the two (or more) holistically opposed positions might be adjudicated, or for some shared experience to which both of us might relate.

Thanks to its ages-old domination of the conversational scene and its appeal as the way most people think they think about war—when they have not thought much about the subject—the just-war tradition as articulated by many Christian thinkers for a millennium and a half is an especially fitting occasion for such a benefit-of-the-doubt explication. Most people who hold to that view have not been pressed to think about it very critically, and many of those in fact believe (wrongly) that there is no other view. Some, as we shall see later, were in fact honoring its logic when in recent times they came to say that they reject it. Others, who say they hold to it and use its vocabulary, do not in fact reason and act accordingly. Thus it would be misleading to attempt to converse with that tradition as if its meaning were clear and univocal before helping it to define itself in such a way as to stand up to challenge and evaluation. It is to that clarification that the present text seeks primarily to contribute.

The preparation of the first version of this book over a decade ago was supported by the faculty improvement program of the University of Notre Dame with aid from the Carnegie Mellon

Foundation, and by the Associated Mennonite Biblical Seminaries with aid from the deFehr Foundation.

I am grateful to Charles Lutz for his pioneering ministry in the concrete implementation of just-war thought in the Lutheran setting during the Vietnam troubles, for his initiative in provoking the conversation to which this book testifies, and for his authorization to re-use his text. I thank Augsburg Press for publishing the first edition of this study, and now for releasing it for this revision. Recognition is owed to Captain King Pfeiffer (ret.) USN PhD for his role in supporting the creation at Notre Dame of a course on the legality and morality of war, where I first was encouraged to study this material, and to Ltc (ret.) US Army Henry J. Gordon and professors Robert Rodes, James Sterba, and Milton Wachsberg for participating in the teaching team.

The project to revise and expand the text was aided by colleagues and students too numerous to name in the Department of Theology and the Joan B. Kroc Institute for International Peace Studies at the University of Notre Dame, by the wise counsel of Robert Ellsberg, by some helpful comments by Robert Rodes and Michael Duffy, and by the editorial assistance of Joseph E. Capizzi. I especially thank Drew Christiansen, S.J., for his willingness to contribute a new response for this edition.

The text proper has been written with a view to readability as a college textbook; at the same time the themes are such as to demand and reward further research. The intention of a study guide like this is to encourage the reader to pursue its themes further. We have therefore provided more annotation than is usual in such a textbook, some topical expositions or study aids condensed in outline form, and some topically specialized bibliographical aids. The annotation thus does not have the ordinary scholarly intention of supporting the points being made, as if they were contested. The literature references and supplementary lists are rather guides for readers who want to find out more. For that reason, the notes are somewhat full. The student using the text proper only as reading for a course need not follow them up.

Foreword to the First Edition

John Howard Yoder has done a good deed for all of us who are a part of the just-war tradition. The essence of his contribution is a simple challenge. As one who stands outside that tradition (but knows it as well as its best inside theorists), Yoder is saying: *If you want me to take you seriously, show me that you take your tradition seriously.*

And it is certainly beyond doubt that those communities which subscribe to the just-war ethic have done little to: (a) teach it to their people; (b) apply it in public policy discussions; and (c) follow its direction when it leads to a conflict with political authority.

Our Record of Neglect

In my own religious tradition, during my lifetime, the record on the teaching of peace/war ethics has been spotty. During the past fifty years U.S. Lutherans have been through peaks and valleys of concern for restraint in the use of armed force.

During the 1930s we had a few who were attracted to the worldwide pacifist movement. The Lutheran Peace Fellowship was formed then, along with numerous other such independent associations within denominations.

With the coming of World War II, however, there was little debate about either pacifism or just/unjust-war ethics, because the need to stop German and Japanese aggression seemed entirely justifiable to most Lutherans. The few who resisted military participation during that war suffered a lonely existence within the Lutheran community.

It is hard to find evidence of serious Lutheran attention to the nuclear weapons debates of the 1950s—in resources for parish education, in the statements of Lutheran church bodies, or in the teaching of the denomination's colleges and seminaries.

A concern for peace/war ethics bloomed among us during the late 1960s and early 1970s, as it did in U.S. society overall, because of the nature of the war in Southeast Asia. Official Lutheran policy statements addressed the morality of the war on the basis of the traditional just/unjust-war theory, and support for selective conscientious objection was first articulated by all major Lutheran church bodies between 1968 and 1970.

Toward the end of the Vietnam War, a major study of the ethics of war and peace in the context of U.S. Lutheranism, *The Witness of U.S. Lutherans on Peace, War, and Conscience,* was produced through the Division of Theological Studies of the Lutheran Council in the U.S.A. On the basis of that document, curriculum for youth and adults on these issues was developed by the church bodies. From 1971 through 1973 the Lutheran Council in the U.S.A. also maintained an office to provide guidance on the draft law in relation to Lutheran ethical understanding.

After the close of the Vietnam War and the ending of the draft, Lutheran interest in peace/war ethics again waned. It did not revive until the early 1980s, with the growing focus on nuclear weapons escalation.

It is on that peak of interest that we stand as this book appears. We have not learned how to sustain a concern for our ethical tradition on war and peace during the times between global crises. We have yet to commit ourselves to consistent peace education among our children, youth, and adults at all times and places in the church's nurturing ministry.

There are two other points I wish to develop in this introduction: (1) the necessity of some moral framework, in addition to pacifism, for dealing with the reality of lethal force; (2) the dilemma of conflict with government to which the just/unjust-war tradition leads.

The Need for a Morality of War

It has become popular in recent decades—especially since the development of atomic and thermonuclear weaponry—for some people to say, "The just-war ethic has outlived its usefulness. In an age of mass-destruction weaponry, the just-war criteria no longer apply."

It has always seemed to me that such statements miss the whole point of the just-war tradition, which is precisely that *because* warfare is terribly destructive and is inclined to escalate into total devastation, there must be a system of restraints, of limits. It is the just-war criteria themselves that, for many nonpacifists today, furnish the tests by which nuclear weapons—and chemical and biological weapons—are declared morally unacceptable.

I believe that any culture that does not adopt the pacifist ethic—and no culture as a whole in today's world has done so—must develop some guidelines restraining the use of force. The alternative is to put into the saddle force itself or those who have most convenient access to force.

An analogy would be that of the police function within our communities. Because of an evident need to protect the innocent and to thwart the destructive impulses of a few, we legitimate the use of force by police officers. We arm them with lethal weapons. We justify their use of such weapons under certain circumstances.

But we do *not* authorize police to use the force at their disposal indiscriminately, arbitrarily, or wantonly. There are rules by which the police must abide. And those rules bear a certain resemblance to the rules of the just-war ethic: use of force must be directed to a specific, limited objective; force must be used in a way that safeguards the innocent; the amount of force must be proportionate to the end sought (don't shoot to kill if you can immobilize); vindictiveness is not permissible; and so on.

The practical alternative to an ethic for restraining the use of lethal force—in domestic police work or in international relations—is not pacifism; it is, rather, unrestrained use of lethal force.

It is exactly at this point that I appreciate the insight of Yoder that the pacifist and just-war traditions "agree most of the time against the other two" positions—the crusade and national-interest wars, neither of which has much room for moral restraint. Before leaving the discussion of the need for a moral framework relating to war, I will suggest three additional reasons why the just-war tradition is useful.

1. *The just-war tradition continues to be the ethical bedrock for a significant body of international law* on the conduct of warfare, for national military manuals on the same subject, and even for the threat of prosecution for war crimes. That is not a small contribution. At least a partial restraint on the destructiveness of war has resulted. *Some* noncombatants have been protected thereby. *Some* forms of weaponry have been declared illegitimate. And *some* military commanders have been deflected from using disproportionate force.

2. *The tradition will be the grounds on which most people who reject nuclear war will do so,* whether they know it or not. They will do it on the basis of simple human rationality, weighing factors that are part of the just-war criteria: the need to limit warfare, the need to protect the innocent (noncombatants or civilians, at the very least children and the elderly). Providing people faced by nuclear weapons with a logical, systematic ethic such as the just-war tradition can be quite a help to the reflection process.

3. *The tradition offers the ethical guidance by which communities of conscience have been helped to make judgments about their participation in or objection to particular military endeavors.* Without something like the just-war tradition, nonpacifists would be adrift with no ethical markers.

Without the just-war tradition, we would immediately set ourselves to inventing something very much like it.

Nothing I have said should be read as a denial that the tradition has obvious weaknesses: it has seldom worked to prevent a war (national leaders are not in the habit of announcing to the world that a war they contemplate is non-justifiable and thus will be abandoned); it assumes fairly complete knowledge of the military and political realities on both sides of a conflict; it is designed for a traditional limited-war situation, where combatants can be cleanly separated from populations as a whole. John Howard Yoder speaks at length concerning these and other weaknesses.

There is, I believe, one additional problem with the ethic of the just war. That is the very name it has carried down through the centuries: just war. The implication is that a given war can be—objectively and theoretically—*just*. This suggests that a war, or war in general, may be viewed as a positive good.

A better term for the tradition would be "war as lesser evil under well-defined circumstances"—but it is clear why such a label never caught on. I normally prefer to speak of a "just/unjust-war ethic" or a "justifiable-war tradition."

No matter what we call it, there will be an abuse of the ethic in the popular mind. The loyal citizen, especially one familiar with our predominant religious traditions, is likely to argue: "Our churches teach a just-war ethic. Our government tells me this is a just war. Therefore, I am obligated to support it." The setting and the tools for rigorously testing whether the proposed war (or war in progress) *is* justifiable—for challenging the government's claim—are simply *not* available to most citizens. Beginnings have been made in applying the tradition's criteria to public-policy debates during the Vietnam War and the current discussion of U.S. nuclear-weapons policy, and for that we should be grateful.

But if the logic of the justifiable-war ethic is to be followed, then the matter of disagreeing with political leadership continues to be an important issue. And that brings us to the second major introductory consideration.

The Disobedience Dilemma

Dr. Yoder suggests that in practice most citizens in nations of the West (those most influenced by the assumptions of the just-war tradition) have followed throughout the centuries and at the present moment continue to follow neither pacifism nor an ethic of justifiable war. In fact, most of us have adhered to a crusader ("this is God's holy war") or a national-interest ("my nation, right or wrong") ethic. I believe he is correct.

One reason it is difficult for us to give more than lip-service to our supposedly orthodox ethic of war is that the just-war tradition inevitably leads to the real possibility of conflict with the law.[1]

We can examine the dilemma by imagining a functioning draft in the midst of some U.S. military enterprise that lacks broad popular support, such as a plan to send combat troops into the oil region of the Persian Gulf or into Central America. Let us suppose that Congress has voted to renew the draft and is inducting large numbers of young American males. Most of them prefer, for reasons of personal convenience, not to be conscripted into armed service. A substantial number, in addition, have learned something of the criteria for justifiable use of armed force as children and youth in their churches and in family discussions. They sincerely believe that their nation's proposed use of their persons in the present context is not justifiable according to the criteria.

Pacifist friends of these young people would have no problem with the government, since objection to participation in all wars is recognized under the draft law. Pacifists must still demonstrate to the draft system that they are sincere, and they will still have to serve in noncombatant roles (either in the military or as civilians) if called. But there is no philosophical reason for conflict between them and the government.

The particular-war objector, however, would have a serious problem under such circumstances. The law does not recognize the right of a citizen to make judgments about the morality of *specific* wars or military enterprises and then to withhold service as a combatant on the basis of such judgments. The irony is that a position held by relatively few of our citizens ("all wars are immoral") is recognized under our draft law as valid; the view supposedly emanating from the religious tradition claimed by the great majority of Americans ("each war must be judged by strict ethical criteria") has no legal status under the draft law.

---

[1] Some of the material in this section is adapted from "The Search for a 'Just Security' Ethic," chapter 11 in Charles P. Lutz and Jerry L. Folk, *Peaceways* (Minneapolis: Augsburg, 1983).

From a practical governmental perspective it is understandable why all-war objectors are excused from service in combat and selective objectors are denied that right. It would be immensely difficult to determine fairly who qualifies and who does not for selective objection—to say nothing of the far larger numbers who could be expected to seek such status.

But there is a profoundly political reason as well why the position of selective participation/objection has found little support among lawmakers. Pacifists do not, in the end, question their own government's policy in undertaking a specific military activity. It is war *itself*, by any nation at any time in history, that is the object of their rejection. Their participation through the bearing of arms is impossible no matter whose war it is or what the cause. Selective objectors, however, are necessarily at odds with a *specific* military policy of their government at a specific time. And that is quite a different matter for the government to address than the perhaps inconvenient but relatively innocuous problem of excusing from combat the few who can persuasively claim a totally pacifist world view.

Ethically speaking, it is rather troubling that we are in such a situation. I would argue that selective participants/objectors who come to a particular military enterprise with careful, conscientious judgments about its morality and then refuse participation on the basis of such moral reasoning are engaging more consciously in moral conduct than are total pacifists. In adopting the position that they can never, under any circumstances, engage in bearing arms, principled pacifists have put the decision *beyond* the realm of moral judgments conditioned by day-to-day circumstances.

Those who seek to follow an ethic such as the just/unjust-war tradition rather than one of universal principle ("all use of armed force is always wrong") are left without a legal place to stand. It is because of this dilemma that the religious communities following a justifiable-war ethic must be very clear: those who run afoul of their own nation's laws because they follow that ethic deserve the fullest support of their churches. To be consistent, those churches ought to advocate change in the conscription law so that selective participation/objection regarding combat service is made legal. But until and unless the law is changed, those churches must stand with their young people who find themselves in civil disobedience out of faithfulness to the ethic they have learned.

This dilemma also should remind us that what is legal and what is moral are not always the same. Law and ethics each have their own logic. Sometimes they will be in conflict.

Conclusion

Some additional observations from the perspective of a Lutheran justifiable-war ethicist may be useful.

1. Yoder points out that the tradition of the just war is not dogma for Roman Catholics but has been given confessional status by Lutherans and other Reformation churches. True, the Lutherans' Augsburg Confession (Article 16) mentions participation in a just war as one of the activities in which Christians may engage. But the point of Article 16 is something else: that Lutherans understand God to be active through the structures of the civil order to bring about justice and peace, and that believers are expected to take part in those structures, such as family and government. Serving as soldiers in a just war is but one illustration, along with paying taxes and marrying. Thus it seems to me that no argument can be made that all Lutherans are bound to adopt the just-war position as their ethic on peace and war. Lutherans are free to opt for pacifism or some other ethic without thereby diminishing their credentials within the Lutheran family. In other words, adherence to the just-war ethic is not a characteristic mark of Lutheran confessionalism in the way that the doctrine of justification by grace and the emphasis on a theology of the cross are commonly understood to be. (I think the same freedom concerning ethics of peace and war is available to Anglicans, Calvinists, and others whose sixteenth-century creeds may mention the just-war tradition.)

2. It is sometimes suggested that people who follow the just/unjust-war approach are likely to be war-oriented or war-accepting. There is clear evidence that genuine adherents to the tradition are resigned to the reality of war in our world and are

eager to do something about both the quantity and the quality of the use of armed force among the nations. But that is not at all the same as to say that just-war theorists are responsible for leading national leaders and peoples into an acceptance of war. As Gary J. Quinn has said, "Proper understanding of just-war theory will no more make one a warmonger than proper understanding of pacifism will turn one into a coward."[2]

3. The essential origin of anything like the just-war ethic, in terms of the biblical faith, is the overarching concern of love for our neighbor. I understand pacifists to begin there also, leading to the argument that violence is never a way to show love to a neighbor, including a neighbor who is our enemy. But I see just-war ethics as being equally concerned with such love. The difference is that another set of neighbors receives primary attention: those who may be called the innocent, those who are in need of protection from attack, those who would be defenseless unless someone took up arms on their behalf. It is finally that question—"How shall the defenseless neighbor be protected?"—that just-war theory is seeking to address. Any other question (such as, "How shall my nation remain supreme in the world?" or "How can the comfortable life-style we have be maintained?") is not a legitimate one for the just-war ethic.

4. The justifiable-war ethic is an ethic for war avoidance or war restraint. It is *not* a set of criteria for building a just peace, that is, a world of peace with justice. I have suggested elsewhere[3] that the churches are called to greater seriousness about constructing a "just-security ethic." While that is a different task than the present book can encompass, the need is obvious. It is also one to which both pacifists and followers of the just-war tradition are drawn if they are serious about ending the violence of war, since ultimately war can be eliminated only through the establishment of conditions that nurture justice, security, and freedom.

5. John Howard Yoder, a pacifist thinker of international renown, is honoring those who stand in the just-war tradition by

---

[2] Gary J. Quinn, "Pacifism and the Just War: Are they Compatible?" *Dialog* (August 1972).

[3] See Lutz and Folk, *Peaceways.*

the pages which follow. He speaks to us as close kin. He is not setting out to denigrate or demolish the just-war ethic. Rather, he is calling us to integrity within the framework of our own claims. He asks us, for the sake of the world, to demonstrate the credibility of our ethic, to put it to the test, to be honest about where it leads us. He remains skeptical, but he is also open to being shown that the just-war ethic *can* make a difference in our time. I am grateful to him for the gift he offers us.

CHARLES P. LUTZ
Director, Office of Church in Society
The American Lutheran Church (1985)
Editor, *Metro Lutheran* (1995)

WHEN WAR IS UNJUST

CHAPTER 1

The Quest to Bring War under Moral Control

The officially dominant view of Christian writers since the early Middle Ages concerning the morality of war has been the so-called just-war tradition. Affirmed implicitly by Ambrose (d. 397) and by Augustine (d. 430), woven into a larger system of moral thought by Thomas Aquinas (d. 1274), and unfolded as a legal/moral system of its own by Francisco de Vitoria (d. 1546) and Francisco Suarez (d. 1617), this teaching appears in the encyclopedias and manuals as the view that most Christians are supposed to hold. It is formally affirmed as binding confessional definition in the official documents of Lutherans (Augsburg Confession, 1530), Anglicans (Thirty-Nine Articles, 1571), and Presbyterians and Congregationalists (Westminster Confession, 1648). It is affirmed as standard by thinkers in denominations that have no creeds (e.g., Baptists).

This tradition can best be defined by contrast, as distinguished:
- from the position of the "realist," who says that it is wrong or impossible to think morally about war;
- from the "pacifist" view, which accepts no war as morally permissible;
- from the "crusading" approach, which believes that with divine backing a war can be "holy";
- and from "macho" or fanatic or "Rambo" attitudes, in which the enemy's humanity does not count and the warrior's "manliness" is self-validating.

The just-war tradition considers war to be an evil, but claims that under certain circumstances it is justifiable, because to en-

1

gage in war would be less evil than to permit the execution of some threat, which it wards off, or the continued existence of some regime that it hopes to change.

It is right that we should, like most scholars recently, speak rather of a "tradition" than of a "theory" or a "just-war doctrine." There is no one official version to which all have subscribed. The tradition, however, is at work wherever:

- a set of criteria is named whereby one can measure political situations,
- with a respectable level of accuracy and objectivity,
- in order to support the case that the evil of a given war, which one "justifies," will be less than the evil of the other war which one thereby prevents.

Later in this book we shall review more fully the criteria that have become prominent in the history of the theme.[1] For our start it suffices to note that they are of several kinds:

- for measuring whether to go to war:
  — the authority waging it must be legitimate;
  — the cause being fought for must be just;
  — the motivation (intention) must be loving;
- for measuring how to apply the decision in a situation:
  — war must be the last resort;
  — success must be probable;
- and for measuring how to fight:
  — the means must be indispensable;
  — the means must be discriminating;
  — the means must respect the provisions of international law.

This listing is only one of many formulations.[2] Often the criteria are grouped in two categories, one governing the choice to go to war (*jus ad bellum*, "the right to fight"), and the other

---

[1] The fullest summary is offered in Appendix V, pp. 147-62 below.

[2] Years ago I randomly surveyed twenty-five lists offered by authors, each of whom assumed that he was describing the general consensus. Yet the lists differed significantly as to how the criteria were stated, how many there were, what exceptions and conditions they were qualified by, and what to do if they were not met. The inclusive listing of criteria in Appendix V was compiled out of all of those lists. It is noteworthy that, in contrast with matters the churches are very concerned about teaching correctly, there is no standard statement of just-war criteria by any ecclesiastical authority.

category governing the prosecution of a war (*jus in bello*, "fighting right").[3]

The just-war position is, as I noted above, the one most Christians say they take. But is that claim accurate? We shall observe that there is reason to doubt that it is. My task is to ask what it would really mean to take a just-war position. As an ecumenical contribution to the integrity and the self-esteem of my just-war interlocutors, I shall proceed to examine the credibility of the dominant tradition.

The Conditions of Credibility

What do we mean when we ask whether a system of ideas is credible?[4] The just-war tradition presents itself as an instrument for making difficult decisions, discerning the morality of violence in the midst of a variety of interpretations. The system comprises a rather long list of criteria, tailored in order to be applicable—on the basis of objective data—to the evaluation of specific conflict situations. The criteria are intended to allow some lethal acts, and to exclude others. There is no question that an affirmative outcome can result from the evaluation; in fact, this is usually the case. What is in question is the possibility of a negative outcome. Can the criteria function in such a way that in a particular case a specified cause, or a specified means, or a specified strategy or tactical move could be *excluded*? Can the response ever be "no"?

This question breaks down into several sub-themes:

1) There will be questions concerning the conceptual adequacy of the system. Are the terms defined in such a way that effective

---

[3] I have sought to add clarity to the structure, going beyond the tradition, by identifying (see pages 154-56) a third set of "procedural" categories that apply both *ad bellum* and *in bello*.

[4] See John Howard Yoder, "The Credibility and Political Uses of the Just War Tradition," *Morals and Might*, ed. George Lopez and Drew Christiansen (Boulder: Westview, 1995) and "The Credibility of Ecclesiastical Teaching on the Morality of War" *Celebrating Peace*, ed. Leroy S. Rouner (Notre Dame, Ind.: University of Notre Dame Press, 1990), 33-51.

implementation could follow when the general criteria encounter real cases?

2) There will be questions concerning the *institutional* requisites for the criteria to operate. Decisions do not crystallize out of the blue; there needs to be some responsible entity or agency with some commonly understood procedures.

3) There will be questions concerning *attitudinal* prerequisites. Facing unpopular facts does not come easy. Discerning when common opinion is deceptive or self-serving is not a kind of thinking for which we are very well trained. What kind of mentality does it take to acknowledge and sustain unwelcome truths against the grain of group pressure or self-interest?

4) There will be questions concerning *moral* requirements. Renouncing morally illegitimate but self-serving acts is costly. Once facts which go against the grain have been discerned, so that to reject a wrong war (or a given wrong act within a war) is imperative, then to *act* at the cost of sure sacrifice demands a special kind of character. What kind of personality will choose the right despite the cost?

5) There may be questions about who *the actor* is. Whose moral decisions are to be illuminated by the just-war tradition? Today we assume that everyone participates in the process: citizen and soldier, as military commander and political actors. Yet in the medieval origins of the tradition, only kings and princes were thought to make moral decisions; citizens had nothing to say, and soldiers had only to obey. Even today some social systems do not grant to everyone the right to decide whether to participate in a war.

In the traditional debate between the proponents and the critics of the just-war tradition, the challenges most often have been of two kinds:

1) Has there ever been a just war that really met the requirements?

2) Has there ever been a party to a conflict—a ruler, government, or general—who rejected an advantageous tactic or strategy on the grounds that it would have been against the rules?

It is certainly a worthy test of any thought system to ask whether it applies to real life. Yet even if there is no perfect case of applicability, the advocates of the just-war tradition can argue that the system has *some* value as an instrument of moral discourse. Like other moral visions that demand a great deal, the validity of the just-war tradition does not depend completely on its being lived up to perfectly.

Why Should a Critic Care?

Why is it worthwhile, from the perspective of an heir and proponent of the Christian pacifist tradition, that a credible just-war discipline be developed?

1) It would serve to confirm the integrity of my interlocutors. There are both Christians and non-Christians who sincerely claim that they are not idolaters sacrificing their fellow creatures to the absolute value of national interest, not frenzied murderers killing without any discipline, not crusaders identifying their cause with God's, but that they limit the violence for which they will soberly accept responsibility to the minimum evil necessary to establish a just peace. I should be and am committed, on general ecumenical or dialogical human grounds, to giving the benefit of the doubt to people who make that claim. Some of them are my friends and colleagues. But for me to take them seriously does demand that I ask of them how they are making that moral claim operational. How do they live up to its demands or even plan to do so?

2) Even though the moral logic with which we reach and justify our decisions is different in general, and directly contradictory at some points, it is still the case that every time just-war proponents exercise effective discipline and limit the harm they do, fewer lives and other values will be destroyed than if they had not applied that restraint.[5] Gordon Zahn, historian of German and Austrian Catholic responses to Hitler, was also challenged to explain what stake a pacifist has in the integrity of just-war thought.[6] His explanation was that as an American

---

[5] We shall have more to say about common adversaries and practical coalitions between pacifism and just war when we reach the 1983 bishops' letter.

[6] "Vietnam and the Just War," *Worldview* 8 (December 1965), 10-12.

Catholic he did not want his church to give its government a blank check for Vietnam as had happened in Hitler's Germany.

3) There will be great progress in conceptual clarification if we can set aside three popular platitudes with which discussion of these matters has been hobbled:

a) The notion that the just-war tradition is the majority view, by which most Christians involved in political responsibility have been living for centuries. In real historical experience, effective adherence to the restraints of the just-war tradition has been and is a rarity.[7] There are persons who say that they hold to such views yet have not developed the tools to make them operational. In fact, most people—and most governments—have engaged without apology in the "realistic" wars of brute national interest or in "holy" or "macho" wars.

b) The notion that the just-war tradition and the pacifist tradition are diametrically opposed. As we shall see, most of the time these positions will agree over against the others. In the face of most real moral choices, whether the ideological "wars of liberation" or the world-threatening nuclear exchange,[8] the two views, if held with integrity, would have the same impact.

c) The notion that acceptance of the just-war view is generally compatible with involvement in responsible political office, whereas pacifism is not. The people who put "just war" in the Protestant creeds of the sixteenth and seventeenth centuries thought that the just-war and pacifist traditions were the only alternatives, which is why they made pacifism a heresy and a crime. Yet just-war criteria are meaningless if they cannot also demand, in particular cases, the refusal of some acts demanded by the national interest. We now have the term *selective conscientious objection* to designate a politically responsible person who refuses a particular activity because it contravenes the just-

---

[7] John Courtney Murray, S.J., "Theology and Modern War," *Theological Studies* 20 (1959), 40-61.

[8] The threat of a major superpower nuclear exchange is less in 1996 than it was when this book was first drafted, yet the threat of nuclear explosives in the hands of rogue powers is greater than it was then. The moral case to be made for any such use is weaker and *still* our country continues to maintain and update a large nuclear stockpile.

war restraints.[9] On the other hand, there are many settings in which pacifists can with full integrity be politically active.

But before leaping to the basic question of credibility, we need a broader acquaintance with what the just-war tradition is about. The tradition is not merely a set of criteria to apply to a political situation. It is as well a culture, shaped by a long history of thought and application, which evolved along the way with more twists and turns than the popularizers or even the theologians tend to acknowledge. Some of our contemporaries think of the just-war tradition as a body of political wisdom which can be utilized without any concern for where it came from. Some Christians, on the other hand, claim that it is authoritative precisely *because* of where it came from, namely from medieval theologians, without any concern for how it has developed since then.

Both answers are too simple. We must study how the tradition evolved before we ask about its present validity, even though our review must be brief. The history of the just-war tradition is well-documented.[10] Meanwhile, the development continues; change is still under way in how the system is interpreted and applied. We shall need to narrate some of those continuing changes, including the landmark study of the Roman Catholic bishops of the United States that led to the pastoral letter *The Challenge of Peace* (1983) and to developments beyond that.[11]

---

[9] See "The Moral Responsibility to Refuse to Serve in Unjust War," Working Paper 3:WP:9. Available from the Joan B. Kroc Institute for International Peace Studies, Notre Dame, IN 46556.

[10] See especially the following books by James T. Johnson, *Can Modern War Be Just?* (New Haven: Yale University Press, 1985); *Ideology, Reason and the Limitation of War: Religious and Secular Concepts 1200-1740* (Princeton, N.J.: Princeton University Press, 1975); (with George Weigel), *The Just War and the Gulf War* (Washington, D.C.: Ethics and Public Policy Center, 1991); *The Just War and Jihad: Historical and Theoretical Perspectives on War and Peace in Western and Islamic Traditions* (New York: Greenwood Press, 1991); *The Just War Tradition and the Restraint of War* (Princeton, N.J.: Princeton University Press, 1981); *The Quest for Peace: Three Moral Traditions in Western Cultural History* (Princeton, N.J.: Princeton University Press, 1987). Among historians there is little debate about the main lines of the story.

[11] See Chapter 7 below and the Afterword by D. Christiansen. It is mostly in these two sections that this book moves beyond the briefer 1984 first edition.

CHAPTER 2

The Just-War Tradition in Its Medieval Context

What we mean by the Middle Ages is not so much a span of time as an arrangement wherein a few assumptions about God and the world were generally shared. The first major teacher of this era, Augustine (d. 430), wrote repeatedly about the just-war concept. He had learned it (as far as this theme is concerned) from his mentor, Ambrose of Milan (d. 397), who in turn had borrowed from the Roman political philosopher Cicero.[1]

The basic assumptions about God and the world that define the Middle Ages are that society as a whole, governed by the civil rulers currently in power and working hand in hand with the bishops and the pope, is in some complex sense "Christian."[2] *Christendom* is a geographic expression, overlapping with the Roman Empire after Constantine (d. 337) and then shrinking to the dimensions of Europe after the Muslim conquests of the seventh and eighth centuries.

Moral thought about social matters will therefore have to be tailored to serve as the religion of an empire, a prince, and later a nation-state. We have to formulate ethics so that an emperor can do what it says. It is in this setting that the just-war tradition was developed; for this reason our account begins with the me-

---

[1] Ambrose had been a powerful civil administrator before he became a Christian and a bishop. His writings follow Cicero's *de officiis* ("On Social Roles"). See Roland Bainton, *Christian Attitudes toward War and Peace* (New York: Abingdon Press, 1960), 90.

[2] Note John Howard Yoder, "The Constantinian Sources of Western Social Ethics," *The Priestly Kingdom* (Notre Dame: University of Notre Dame Press, 1984), 135-50.

8

dieval synthesis in order to observe what the tradition meant concretely when it first became dominant.[3]

Few Citizens Participate

Involvement in the regrettable but unavoidable military violence authorized by the medieval tradition was not permitted to most people. Such authorization was given to the prince, whose status was defined by the criteria of legitimate authority (which usually meant by inheritance) and to those under his command.

For economic reasons soldiers were few. There was a small number of knights, whose definition of their role included honor—fighting fair and defending the innocent. Second, there was a larger but fluctuating number of mercenaries, recruited only when needed. Both groups had a right to fight when and because the prince had that right. The mercenaries had no personal moral preference as to which side should win, except for the pay, the privileges of plunder, the enjoyment of a good fight, and the desire to stay alive. The knights had high moral standards, but they too could put their skills at the service of any ruler.

In emergencies, local militia could be called up for defense in times of immediate threat, but not as instruments of policy on a larger-than-local scale. The yeoman was an intermediate category, less than a knight and more than a serf, whose landholding privileges included his being in the first line for battle service.

The common folk, with no skills and no weapons, were exempt from regular military service obligations. The modern notion of the ordinary citizen being patriotically devoted to national service did not exist. Instead, the prince's ordinary subjects, including most able-bodied males, usually were not considered apt for military service. The prince had the legal right to call them to war, but he did so only rarely, since they were needed in the fields or in their trades in order to bring in the tax money to pay for the war. There were well-elaborated moral theories to inter-

---

[3] The just-war tradition never "became dominant" in the sense that most of the baptized, or most rulers, respected it. The theologians who articulated it are our sources.

pret why most people (*subjects* rather than *citizens*) should not be combatants. But if the prince did demand their services, they were not expected to have minds of their own.

Other categories were forbidden to fight, even in local self-defense. This included pilgrims and penitents, the religious and the secular clergy, with the very special exception of the military monks who, although under religious vows, were primarily knights.[4] Thus the people allowed to fight in a just war were a small minority of the population. The others were expected, just as much as before Constantine, to renounce bloodshed and to accept suffering as part of the Christian way.

The Bishops as Peacemakers

The primary impact of the medieval church as an institution on war as an institution was not in the room its moral teaching made for justifiable war, but rather in the framework of other measures of restraint, taken often by local bishops and occasionally by higher authorities (councils, synods and popes).

The Peace of God[5] was a "spatial" measure, a law pronounced by a bishop or a regional council, which assigned special spiritual status to certain places, where there should be no fighting, or to certain persons (pilgrims, clergy, peasants in their fields), who should be left out of the hostilities. Not only the church building and the cemetery were exempt. Often the lands and the flocks of a monastery or hospital were out of bounds for war.

The Truce of God was a "temporal" measure, also proclaimed by a bishop or a synod, whose authority did not depend on the agreement of the parties (as *truce* ordinarily means), providing

---

[4] The Teutonic Knights were founded in 1189 and militarized by German bishops and princes in 1198. The Knights Templar began circa 1120 under Baldwin II, king of Jerusalem; in 1139 they were placed under the authority of Pope Innocent II. The Knights of Malta started in the eleventh century as a hospital order founded by Italian merchants in Jerusalem. By the early twelfth century they were a formidable military order.

[5] The term was a standard canonical one at the time (see Bainton, *Christian Attitudes Toward War and Peace*, 110-12).

that during certain periods (Sunday, holy days, Lent, a specific cooling-off period) there should be no hostilities.

It is not clear how much these limitations decreased the carnage, since medieval military operations raised great challenges for supply and transportation, rest and recuperation. Nevertheless, these measures made publicly evident, in terms which everyone could grasp and respect, that the church wanted war to be limited, and that Christian people, even when authorized to make war, were obligated to do it within defined restraints.

Finally, bishops often led in aggressive mediatorial efforts. They intervened as peacemakers between neighboring princes in order to reduce the destruction.[6] Sometimes they reinforced these initiatives by imposing spiritual sanctions.[7]

Legitimate Does Not Mean Good

By *legitimate* we mean "in conformity with the rules." Legitimate is less than good, as justified is less than just. War is an evil, a harm, which in a special case may be admitted for the sake of some other value it defends. It is not a good in itself.

The social setting in which the just-war tradition developed most substantially was not that of a king consulting his advisors, looking at a possible military adventure to decide on its advisability or legitimacy. The patterns of governmental decision-making before democratic times did not include that kind of openness about how decisions are made and why. Just-war thinking was done in the confessional, and in the studies of the priests who developed canon law. The criteria were needed when a knight or soldier returned from battle, and the question was whether he could be admitted to the eucharist, and what difference it made in that connection whether the war in which he had

---

[6] Bainton enumerates such negotiations (*Christian Attitudes toward War and Peace*, 116ff.). In the Catholic-dominated world this is still a live possibility. In May 1985 Vatican mediation resolved a long-standing border conflict between Chile and Argentina. In January 1994 the Bishop of Chiapas brought the government of Mexico into conversation with the Zapatista rebels.

[7] The *interdict* was a measure suspending the celebration of the eucharist in a territory whose sovereign was guilty of infractions.

killed was "just" or not.[8] The point at which the detailed just-war rules were worked out the most thoroughly was thus the determination of the form and type of penance called for after killing.

Even for killing in a just cause some period of penance was demanded; even for killing in a just cause a candidate for the priesthood could be rendered ineligible to receive orders. In fact, those restrictions applied to those whose participation in killing went no farther than serving in a jury that condemned someone to death.

Holy Does Not Mean Just

Under the category of just cause, earlier authors included two quite distinct kinds of warrant: 1) properly political matters, such as a direct attack, the seizure of territory, or unpaid debts, and 2) what we would call religious matters, such as punishing the offense of blasphemy or a divine command to destroy some enemy. These two kinds of warrant called for different kinds of reasoning, and toward the end of the Middle Ages some thinkers began to disentangle them. The same terms were used to describe both, but different kinds of moral argument were developing, with the "holy" war coming to be distinguished from the "properly political" justifiable war.[9]

Crusade is the Christian term for a "holy" war. The concept was present in other religious cultures, in ancient Israel, and in Islam as well. Some modern ideological or ethnic visions (manifest destiny, leninism, fascism) may have the same moral structure. We can characterize the difference between "holy" and "justified" at several points:

---

[8] The most substantial study in this realm is Frederick H. Russell, *The Just War in the Middle Ages* (Cambridge. Cambridge University Press, 1975).

[9] This is not to say that the two realms did not overlap. Until the seventeenth century in Northern Europe, and still longer elsewhere, provision for the promotion of true religion was considered one of the proper roles of government.

a) The cause has a transcendent validation. What is at stake is not a finite political value that needs to be weighed over against other political values, so that the clash of interest of the various parties in the social mechanism can be subjected to a careful calculus of proportionality. The commander and the warriors are freed from such political calculations by the overarching value of the holy cause.

b) This transcendent quality is known by revelation. The decision does not arise from soberly measuring a situation. Diplomats do not define it. It comes to us from beyond the picture we ourselves have of our setting. Ordinarily this information "from beyond" comes from a special person or institution: a guru, a prophet, an ayatollah, or an oracle. Moses and Joshua took orders directly from God. In churches with a strong institutional frame, the validation may come from a pope or a council. For instance, the famed abbot Bernard of Clairvaux preached the first Crusade.

c) The adversary has no rights, or at least no vested rights that have to be respected. Some Crusaders made exceptions and did not kill women and children, but often in holy war genocide is the norm. In the Iberian invasion of South America this dimension surfaced in the claim of some that the natives had no human souls, or that even if they were human they had no rights. Often this attitude correlates with racist or ethnic deprecation or depreciation of the enemy ("the only good Indian [or Viet Cong or whatever] is a dead one"). Restraint is no virtue; excess may be a proof of devotion.

d) The criterion of last resort does not apply. Other ways of working toward the same goal (accepting half a loaf as better than nothing, mediation, compromise, etc.) are dishonorable in the face of the transcendent [duty to destroy.]* *because*

e) Success need not be probable. To fail in a holy cause can be a moral victory. To die in a holy war is the shortest way to heaven. Even in the modern analogues there is a kind of immortality assigned to martyrs, as seen in the special status of the memory of Che Guevara or Sandino, or the mystique of suicide bombing in the Japanese air forces in World War II, or, more recently, in Near Eastern terrorism.

Once the concept of the holy war has been defined with some clarity, it drops out of our present study *for purposes* of.Christian moral discourse. No Roman Catholic bishop has proclaimed a crusade since the Middle Ages.[10] The questions raised by thinking that there can be such a transcendently righteous war are quite different from the ones we shall be pursuing in the rest of this book. Yet for purposes of historical honesty we must acknowledge that this kind of thought has not dropped out of our world. The "survival of the free world" or the "liberation of the proletariat" can constitute transcendent-cause claims that are not subject to political measurement, so that the "holy" mentality is still at work.

The Moral Autonomy of the State

Toward the end of the medieval period a different line of reasoning developed. It had always been present, but it took the Renaissance to bring it to the surface.[11] Machiavelli (d. 1527) gave his name to the claim that the prince is the only judge and the only locus of value in his nation. The interest of the prince, the regime, is the only binding appeal, whether we argue that it is moral, immoral, or amoral. Moral language can still be used in a subordinate way, as one of the tools of politics, sometimes to get people to keep their promises to the prince and to make them think he is a good man. Yet obligations to tell the truth or to keep promises or to respect the sanctity of life are never absolute; if the welfare of the ruling house can be served, those values may be sacrificed in particular cases.

When Machiavelli spelled out the autonomy of value he claimed for the power and welfare of the prince, that counted over against three alternative interests:

• The rights and desires of his own people;

---

[10]The concept is, of course, still operational within Islam, and it has had rough equivalents in Marxism and fascism. The term *crusade* is used in a loose way by many.

[11]Hugo Grotius and Michael Walzer trace its roots back to the ancient Greeks.

- The rights and desires of <u>others</u> to whom he may have obligations;
- The rights and values of the <u>moral order</u>—if there is such a thing, whether thought of as defined by priests or by philosophers or just as present there in the nature of things.

The first two of these were most obvious for Machiavelli and his first readers, but the third concerns us more. Here we are considering the morality of war, not the rights of citizens. The claim that the interest of the regime is an autonomous value, subject to no higher adjudication, is an issue independent of the autocratic and aristocratic impact of Machiavelli in his own time. Modern Western political theory, called realist by some, affirms the accountability of governments to their own people yet makes the interest of each government autonomous in its relations to other nations.[12]

The notion of the divine right of kings has often been another label for the style Machiavelli advocated. Here, ultimate moral authority is located in the ruler, but that fact is divinely sanctioned, not as an exception or exemption from God's control but as revelation in its own right.[13]

Thus the autonomy of the national interest, as a moral value in itself, has emerged as a distinctive type of reasoning, neither pacifist nor "just war." <u>It denies either explicitly or implicitly the possibility that the military operations of the state could or should be judged in the light of objective criteria other than self-interest.</u> That means a rejection of just war in the strict sense.[14] It

---

[12]The concepts of society, people, nation, state, and regime are all different in what they mean as moral actors, yet the same argument works for all of them in the sense that Machiavellianism frees them from having to exercise legal or moral restraint in behalf of the rights of others.

[13]There were other, more demanding understandings of "divine right" that made the ruler subject to God's moral demands as interpreted by the bishop or the theologian, but generally such views were not held by rulers.

[14]This notion of autonomy is identified as such, although without the name "realism," in the first chapter ("Prolegomena") to Grotius's *On the Laws of War and Peace.* Michael Walzer's use of the term "realism," and placing it in "scare quotes" to signal that its clarity and value can be challenged, has influenced standard usage.

differs from the holy war in that the interest of the prince or the state claims no higher validation.

Although the bluntness with which Machiavelli had spelled out the principle of unabashed selfishness offended some, not long after his time many who considered themselves morally very serious accepted a similar notion under the heading "national sovereignty." The end of feudal networks and of Christendom as an empire, in favor of strong independent nations, was accepted by most currents of opinion as a step forward. For Machiavelli, it was the prince who needed to take no fundamental account of the rights of others. Now it came to be "the nation" as a body, or even "the people," yet that autonomy was incarnated especially in the ruling house or the government (however it was selected). National sovereignty was supposed to rank above the world solidarity, whether that of a faith group, an ethnic group, or humanity as a whole, for all citizens. The concrete effect of the notion of national solidarity was to make a particular authoritarian government exempt from deep criticism, yet somehow at the same time it was claimed that it represented the dignity and freedom of all the nation's people. A particular ruling elite thus evades criticism by saying it serves the nation, and the capacity of anyone to challenge the moral autonomy of any government on its own territory is radically circumscribed.

Thus it is that since the Middle Ages there have been three distinct modes of nonpacifist logic available, each of them used by morally serious thinkers, even though they are hardly separated in patriotic discourse or day-to-day politics: national interest, holy war, and the war that is justified in the particular case by authentically political but morally restrained warrants.[15]

There has been yet another mode of thought in our culture, not used by morally serious thinkers but powerful in politics, entertainment, and in real human conflicts: the "macho" or "Rambo" view. One fights in order to prove one's manhood. In

---

[15]This tripartite logical analysis will need to be further refined later to take account of the impacts of the Protestant Reformation, the rise of international law, the rise of the modern nation, and the power of less rational styles.

battle it may be called frenzy or excess killing or passion; in politics it may be called strength. It sells in our culture. A person's manly dignity is confirmed by his disregard for the human dignity of his adversaries. Theologians seldom take account of the cultural power of this alternative.

Justifiable Is Not Sinless

The interpreters with whom we are conversing are agreed that *justifiable* is a more precise adjective than *just*, since no claim is made that the destruction involved in a justifiable war is itself a positive good. The mainstream of the tradition does not say that such military actions are morally imperative, that they glorify God, but only that a case can be made for them and that those who find that they must do them are not to be treated as morally irresponsible. Some adherents would still say that the actions committed in the just war are sinful in a profound sense and constantly stand in need of forgiveness. Others would reject the characterization as "sinful"[16] but would still describe the destruction worked by a justifiable war as materially evil, not as good.

The moral thinkers who developed this body of tradition, both the confessors and canon lawyers measuring the gravity of particular offenses and the writers of systems closer to the end of the period, did not see themselves as triumphalists or as making a case for the politics of establishment, blessing whatever their rulers were doing. Most of them were fundamentally sad about the difference between the City of God and the "city of man." As Roland Bainton commented, the concession that killing could not be avoided can be morally valid (in Augustine) only when it is "mournful," a concession rather than a mandate, a regrettable duty rather than an intrinsically righteous obedience.

Ambrose used his justifiable-war tradition (and his own considerable experience as a lay political authority before he be-

---

[16]In the past generation this was clearly said by Paul Ramsey. Ramsey's contributions to the just-war tradition are voluminous (see Bibliography).

came a Christian and a bishop) as leverage to motivate and articulate a concrete critical focus against injustices committed by his emperor, Theodosius.[17] At the other end of the Middle Ages we shall see Vitoria doing something similar. Thus the just-war tradition was the officially dominant though not the only moral guidance addressed to the public life in the early Middle Ages.

---

[17]When the Emperor Theodosius had trapped some seven thousand citizens of Salonica in a hippodrome and massacred them as punishment for disrespect, Ambrose threatened him with excommunication and obliged him as penance to spend several nights on his knees in the cathedral of Milan.

CHAPTER 3

Weakening the Just-War Restraints

The medieval origins of the just-war tradition are far from our age; we need to turn to surveying how the just-war tradition grew over the centuries. There naturally will be both intellectual and institutional changes to chronicle.

The story is complicated and can be told only in broad strokes. Rather than seeking to detail events and thoughts year by year and place by place, it will have to suffice to identify the major strands that stretch through the story from early times to the last century. It will be simplest to group in one chapter the causes that favored effective restraint, and in another (this one) the causes pushing in the other direction. Thus the order of presentation will not be simply chronological.

The Protestant Reformation[1]

The massive political and ecclesiastical movements that swept northern Europe during the sixteenth century are usually grouped together as "the Reformation." They left behind a Christendom divided four ways. In Britain, in the countries along the Rhine from the Netherlands to Switzerland, and from Scandinavia to Hungary in the East, there arose the Anglican, Lutheran, and

---

[1] For a more complete discussion of this subject, see John Howard Yoder, "The Reception of the Just War Tradition by the Magisterial Reformers," *History of European Ideas* 9:1 (1986).

Reformed (or Calvinist) traditions, each supported and governed by some national governments.

The common Protestant assumption is that the just-war tradition was one of the few points where the Catholic position was taken over with the least change, but that is not quite what happened. Several dimensions of the situation changed in such a way that, counter to the reformers' intentions, the potential of the just-war concepts for applying restraint was decreased.

Each of the three movements was ruled by the state in its respective territory (the king or queen in England, the territorial princes where Luther led, and city-state governments where the Reformed pattern prevailed). Each retained the baptism of infants (i.e., involuntary membership, keeping church membership identical with citizenship) and the approbation of war. Theologians in the universities and pastors in the parishes were accredited and paid for by princes and city councils. The three systems differed in some details of doctrine and structure, but they had in common the conviction that it was not only permissible but mandatory that the church should be structured at the initiative of civil government and that all the citizens of a given province should have the same religion.

This made it much less likely than it had been in the Middle Ages that a theologian or a pastor might provide a critical moral perspective on decisions made by his ruler, who was at the same time his employer. An exceptionally courageous Huldrych Zwingli (in Zurich) or John Knox (in Scotland) could sometimes bite the hand that fed him, but such independence was not typical. In fact, when Knox or Zwingli criticized their governments, it was often in the other direction, asking for *more* rather than less violence to be used in both civil and religious matters than the rulers thought wise.

The status of the just-war tradition was also changed by its being given creedal status. The 1530 Augsburg Confession (Lutheran), the 1561 Thirty-Nine Articles (Anglican), and the 1648 Westminster Confession (Reformed) all affirm the "just war." Some of them expressly condemn any who think otherwise. In the Roman Catholic setting, on the other hand, it would never have occurred to Augustine or Thomas to define such matters as dogma. They took just-war reasoning for granted, assumed as part of the self-evident consensus, but to doubt such reasoning was not heresy. There has never been a normative statement by a pope or a council to make acceptance of this doctrine obligatory for Catholics.[2] Thus no dogmatic definition has stood in the way of the resurgence of pacifism among Catholics in recent decades.[3] On the other hand, the just-war tradition is theoretically obligatory for Protestants of those majority traditions where the Reformation was implemented by a government and fixed in a confession.

Perhaps more weighty, when measured in terms of psychological impact, was the removal of exceptions. No longer were clergy, the religious, pilgrims, and penitents exempted from war. Such persons were thought by the reformers to represent the false notion of salvation by works and the spiritual privilege of religious status, which the Reformation swept away. Special persons, special times (like the Truce of God), and special places (like the Peace of God) were no longer respected. Previously the prince and his soldiers were exceptions to the general rule of nonviolence, which was normally binding on most people most of the time. Now the state's violence is the norm, the definition, even when not all are called to fight.

The Protestant Reformation also provided new occasions for righteous violence. The Reformation itself needed to be defended by force of arms. The Protestant status of a particular province, on which the freedom of preaching depended, became a new "just cause." For the next century many wars had a religious component. Religious differences coincided with and accelerated the breakup of Europe into separate sovereign nations, giving such new divisions religious sanction. It had been decided that the religion of the province should be determined by that of the sovereign.[4] In effect, the prince functioned as a bishop.[5]

---

[2] This was noted in an editorial in *La Civilta Cattolica*, see below page 93.

[3] Ronald C. Musto, *The Catholic Peace Tradition* (Maryknoll, N.Y.: Orbis Books, 1986); Patricia McNeal, *Harder than War* (New Brunswick, N.J.: Rutgers University Press, 1992).

[4] This came to be expressed in the phrase *cujus regio, ejus religio* ("whose is the rule, his is the religion"); the principle, if not the phrase, was decided upon in the 1555 Peace of Augsburg between Catholic and Lutheran princes.

[5] Martin Luther used the term "emergency bishop" to describe the prince's role in reforming the church.

Now that every church had a state and every state a church, the only means to defend or advance a religious cause was military or diplomatic. So Europe saw a series of wars of religion, bringing into the heartland of Christendom the escalation of religious claims previously reserved for hostilities against the infidel. Just when Catholic tradition had begun to disentangle the no-holds-barred crusade from the civilly justified but also restrained war,[6] internecine battles restored to the heart of Christendom the reality of the crusade without the name. During the Thirty Years' War (1618-1648) half of the middle of Europe was destroyed in the name of God.

Not only did the Reformation bring about wars *between* nations on the grounds of confessional difference, but it also provided the basis for an escalation of the notion of righteous revolution *within* a nation. The idea that there could be a moral justification for not remaining subject to a government, on the ground that it was a bad government, was present already in the thought of Thomas Aquinas,[7] but there it figured only as an intellectual exercise. Thomas did not illustrate with real cases. Neither Thomas nor the lawyers of his time had spelled this out in real cases, but the Reformation did, because if the ruler was on the wrong side theologically, his concern for the peace of his province meant preventing the proclamation of the word of God. Responding to the massacre of St. Bartholemew's night (1573) in France and to the Inquisition in the (Spanish) Netherlands, Reformed theologians developed in numerous tracts a theory of righteous revolution. They called it *tyrannicide*, but what identified the ruler as a tyrant was not bad government in general but his opposing the Reformation.[8] It was assumed, as it had been by Thomas, that the tyrant was one bad person; if he were

---

[6] We shall observe this development in the next chapter.

[7] Aquinas's way of saying it was that sedition is always a sin; but when a ruler is very bad it is that bad ruler who is guilty of sedition, and the people who rise up against him represent good government (*Summa Theologica*, II-II Q. 43, art. II, reply 3).

[8] The main Huguenot authors were Hubert Languet (d. 1581), François Hotman (d. 1590), and Philippe Dupplessis-Mornay (d. 1623), author of *Vindiciae contre tyrannos* (in English translation, London 1648). Collectively they were called *monarchomanes*. Jesuits wrote similar treatises about assassinating Queen Elizabeth.

removed, good government would snap back, thus minimizing the suffering. In a quite parallel way Catholic writers developed the theoretical justification for the assassination of Queen Elizabeth.

Yet before long this focus on removing the one bad ruler grew into a theory of government as covenant, claiming that the ruler possessed his or her authority in the first place only by virtue of a reciprocal understanding with the rest of the nobles.[9] Therefore the subjects' duty to submit was conditional, subject to revocation by virtue of the ruler's bad performance. And what worse performance could there be than forbidding the true religion? The independence of Scotland and the independence of the Netherlands were founded on this kind of claim.

Thus the roots of social-contract theory reach back well beyond the age of Enlightenment to the Reformation and Counter-Reformation theories of righteous insurrection. These theories set aside in one further way the initial restraining effect of the just-war tradition.

Enlightenment

The second wave of cultural change we need to follow is the one we call Enlightenment. Here the value of the nation becomes secularized, freed from religious sanctions, criteria, and controls. This secularization of states, or disenfranchisement of churches, arose from a kind of antimilitary critique, fed by disgust with the way in which religious motivations had driven the rulers of Europe into self-destructive combat. Politics was to be made more modest, reduced to functional utility rather than crusading. Yet with the same blow the values of the nation, whereby "utility" would be measured, became autonomous and materialistic; they were withdrawn from the purview of moral criticism by the theologians and the churches. Thus by limiting the likelihood of a

---

[9] This is a quite proper understanding on the basis of the way feudal society had developed. To call a society "feudal" means that its order is based upon a reciprocal oath (*foedus*) binding a superior and a subordinate party. If the superior party fails to discharge the promises to provide peace and justice, the vassal can be freed from the covenant. Later Reformed thought provided that the "lesser magistrates" would have the authority to rebel.

crusade, Enlightenment humanists increased the power of a Machiavellian prince.

One mark of political criticism in this age was the growing theoretical importance of the citizen and of the social covenant as a basis for the effort to rein-in the uncontrolled authority of rulers. Yet the more we call on a ruler to be accountable to the people, the easier it is for both ruler and people to take less account of the rest of the world community and the rights of other nations. Demagogic campaigns of hatred or suspicion against other nations became one way for a ruler to stir up support and divert criticism.

The notion of revolution was also secularized. For the revolutionary thinkers of the sixteenth century, the offense that made a king worthy of being unseated was failure to permit preaching of the gospel or the practice of the faith. But with the age of Enlightenment, the criteria for declaring a regime unworthy of loyalty could be drawn from political philosophy or ideology. These matters are even more difficult to define and adjudicate with any objectivity than *religious truth*. Every political doctrine can accredit some spokespersons to proclaim that a specific regime has forfeited its legitimacy. What had begun with the criticism of royalty by a few elite philosophers in the seventeenth century became in the eighteenth century a blank check for almost any ideologue to call for the violent end of almost any regime.

Total War

A third major early modern development is that war became total in a number of different ways, each of them decreasing the possibility of effective restraint. These changes arose most rapidly in the age of revolution, especially in France. (See Appendix II, pages 130-35 below.)

With this development, every citizen is claimed as a supporter of the cause. The revolution's rhetoric claims that it restructures society in the name of all "the people." Thus every citizen is a partisan and there is no room for neutrality. War is no longer between princes, or royal houses, or dynasties, but between nations as wholes. Since every citizen is a partisan, there is no longer the same meaning to the thought that citizens should be treated as noncombatants.

Hand in hand with the change in ideology went changes in the management of the political system. It became possible to mobilize almost everyone. *Every* citizen is a soldier. Wars are won less by position, which can depend on a decisive battle, and more by attrition, which depends on the total strength of the enemy's economy. Thus, the economy can be manipulated in such a way that even civilian productivity is understood as contributing to the war effort. Everyone is in some sense a combatant, not only in the moral sense of being emotionally committed to the national cause, but also as part of a unified war economy. No longer is the warrior class a select minority with an elite ethos.

Not only is the entire population economically mobilized, but all able-bodied citizens may be subject to being called up as soldiers. The Napoleonic age generalized the use of a standing army of ordinary soldiers drawn from the entire population, or at least from most of the lower social strata, by obligation rather than by lifelong profession. This created a new relationship between the population and the army, and thereby between the population and the government. It also weakened the notion that the military ethos of "fighting fair," a mark of nobility, can be expected of ordinary soldiers.

Technological Escalation

The above three changes coincided and overlapped with a fourth. The technologies of manufacturing, transportation, and communication expanded exponentially the capacity to destroy and the speed with which it could be done. Before Napoleon, a war involved delays of weeks, during which troops had to move on foot from one front to the other. Diplomats could move more rapidly than soldiers and arms, so notions of last resort were meaningful. Now, all such notions dealing with timing and due process need redefinition. Discrimination and immunity likewise no longer have simple meanings.

The notion that the state represents all of the people rather than being an aristocracy by divine right would at first seem to provide new leverage to be critical of military adventurism, since those who die tend to be of the people rather than the elite who make the political decisions. Pacifist arguments have often spoken of war as the activity of aristocrats, whom the common people should refuse to support. Yet seldom (before recent generations) did the people echo that critique. Democracy seems rather to have increased the space for demagoguery.

In order to gain a popular mandate and seem stronger than their adversaries, politicians may exploit nationalistic and xenophobic, even racist, enthusiasms of common folk, thereby putting themselves under pressure to perform in a way as "patriotic" as their campaign language. Once the battle has begun and lives have been given, it is far more difficult to contemplate suing for peace. The medieval vision of the prince as a responsible and wise decision-maker, able to lead his people because he knew more of the facts, had studied the craft of governing, and had the courage and also the power to make unpopular but right choices, is replaced by elected politicians who become the captives of the patriotic sentiments and short-circuited analyses their own campaigning stirred up. The medieval monarch could, if wise, cut the losses and make peace. Democratic leaders may be less free to be wise, especially once they have cranked up the fervor for war. Whether we speak of the relatively genuine democracies, in which popular suffrage is effective, or of the many places in which the facade of an electoral process is used to cover less worthy policies and less valid processes of decision, it often appears that to involve the masses in decisions about war and national honor does not provide for a more effective defense of the real interests of most of the people. The issues at stake are subject to rapidly changing moods and to deceptive rhetoric. Decisions about whether to have a war, about what, and how long are not made more wisely just because there are elections. Democratic forms may well work against restraint.

A further escalation, of a different kind, arises as a change in the notion of justified revolution. We saw before that the concept of revolution as a subset of just war had earlier roots; now the components of the argument change. The claims that can count as just cause against a ruler accused of tyranny tend to escalate in the age of democracy. The claims are easier to make and harder to criticize.

The revolutions of 1776 and 1779 spoke of freedom in ways whose meaning was simple, whether the people removed a monarchical regime in their own country, as in France, or seceded from an empire, as with the American colonies. However, in many cases in the last two centuries, the claim for revolution made by the combatants has tended to become "total." Careful measurements of just cause or of intention, proportion, or probable success are not provided. The authority to destroy one regime in the name of a different one, or to sacrifice present peace for the sake of a better future, comes to be based not on the votes of citizens but on some ideological cause. The escalation is both quantitative and qualitative. Whether on the right or the left, the revolutionary politics of the twentieth century claims a higher level of validation than in the eighteenth, and therefore is even more difficult to measure by moral criteria. In other words, modern revolutions tend to become not justifiable but holy wars.[10]

An obvious example of such a "holy" escalation has been the claim of some kinds of Marxism that a particular subversive group is above moral questions concerning just authority or probable success, since the revolution is by its definition the right side to be on, at whatever cost. The same may be going on when "the defense of the free world" is considered to be an unchallengeable justification for anything that a government (or a rebel) claims a mandate to do.

Military Necessity

The notion of military necessity means in ordinary parlance that an otherwise valid restriction may be disregarded when it

---

[10]This escalation may be linked to the presence of democracies. If electoral procedures exist whereby the people can change their rulers, then to make a case for revolution one must deny the authenticity of the democratic structures, accusing them of corruption such that they do not really represent the people.

impedes effectiveness. We may break the rules if we "have to" for some valid national end.

On the other hand, for strict constructionists like Francis Lieber, author of the 1863 "General Orders" prepared at Abraham Lincoln's request to guide soldiers in civil war, the question of "necessity" is a hard question, a restriction, and not a blank check. Even among the kinds of damage that the rules of war permit, one may only inflict those indispensable to winning:

> Military necessity, as understood by modern civilized nations, consists in the necessity of those measures which are *indispensable for securing the ends* of war, *and which are lawful* according to the modern law and usages of war [emphasis added].[11]

The drift is strong toward the more permissive use of the term *necessity*; it increasingly has come to mean that one may legitimately break the rules whenever one "really has to," which tends to boil down to being useful (saving lives, shortening the war) rather than to the real lack of any other means.[12]

The most widely noted use of this kind of argument has been connected with massive city bombing, since the infraction against noncombatant immunity is the most obvious. The argument that the dropping of the atomic bomb over Hiroshima ultimately saved lives by shortening the war became very prominent in the public

---

[11] "General Orders No. 100" (1863), Article 14. The same provision is argued in *The Law of Land Warfare, Field Manual FM 27* 1956, paragraph 1/1/3/a, page 4.

[12] This observation is made both by the international lawyer Telford Taylor, in his article "War Crimes" (425ff.), and by the political philosopher Richard Wasserstrom in "The Laws of War" (455ff.), both reproduced in Malham M. Wakin, ed , *War, Morality, and the Military Profession* (Boulder: Westview, 1979). Michael Walzer rejects this loose usage, yet still holds open a narrow space for a "supreme emergency," which may allow some infractions without justifying them, when the stakes are very high (*Just and Unjust Wars* [New York: Basic Books, 1977; 2d ed. 1992], 245-55 [1st ed.]; other references see index).

debate in the United States in 1995.[13] It is also in this connection that Michael Walzer used the notion of "supreme emergency" to discuss the case for bombing German cities.[14]

Other Dimensions of the Inability to Control

Centering most of our attention on the nuclear threshold from 1945 to the 1980s has hidden from many people another qualitative change that was just as fundamental in essence, and in fact more real. The war waged in Algeria by the French (1955-1963), the one in Vietnam by the French in the 1950s and then by the Americans until 1975, or those supported by the United States in Central America, were a new kind of war, at least in their breadth and intensity.[15]

Guerrilla war is morally problematic on the revolutionary side because those who prosecute the war cannot, almost by definition, prove objectively that they are the "legitimate authority" representing the people. They have to accredit themselves by appeal to the cause they represent or to the political doctrine they promise to implement. They have to whip their own people into line with very severe internal enforcement, if not terrorism. They make enemies of their own compatriots who have not yet

---

[13] See Gar Alperowitz, *Atomic Diplomacy: Hiroshima and Potsdam* (New York: Simon & Schuster, 1975; London: Penguin, 1985; London and Boulder: Pluto Press, 1995). This very noisy and highly politicized debate lost sight of the fact that shortening the war and saving combatant fatalities at the expense of intentionally taking civilian lives would not be legitimate *even if* the calculation were accurate.

[14] The concept occurs frequently in Walzer's *Just and Unjust Wars*. If in fact the survival of the free world is at stake, the bombing of innocent urban populations may be what a government should do, although the general who did it should not be decorated.

[15] Some have used *low intensity* to describe these wars, because the size of combatant groups may be small or the arms limited. Yet in terms of suffering, social stress, and actual lives lost, these forms of decentralized, low-visibility wars may be just as destructive.

joined the liberation forces, and thereby undermine their claim to legitimacy rather than strengthen it.

On the other side, anti-guerrilla warfare is harder to justify both legally and morally than a classical war against an invader. The government that defends itself against strong internal opposition would probably not win a fair election. Often, as was the case in Vietnam, the regime claiming legitimacy is internally corrupt, politically without vision, and economically or militarily the puppet of outside forces. Further, the nature of the conflict makes it extremely difficult to respect civilian immunity.

Thus, when moral thinkers want to adjust to this new kind of war,[16] the just-war criteria that are selected for application and for writing into law[17] are not those which reinforce restraint, but those that are most easily transposed into a less demanding set of rules that can be kept. Others are tacitly neglected because their measurement would be impossible or their enforcement difficult, or because it is not clear that both parties in the conflict would have an equal interest in accepting such restrictions.

Conclusion

Even one of the above changes is sufficient to make the applicability of the just-war tradition questionable. When taken cumulatively, they have hollowed out the tradition to little more than a shell. The words are still there, but the realities to which they apply escape almost entirely the discipline that used to be, if not effective, at least reasonably thinkable. The shell has been retained, while what goes on beneath it is quite different from what the theologians who initially found the just-war tradition convincing could ever have meant or would ever have approved.

It was thus not at all over-reaction when Jesuit theologian John Courtney Murray, writing in 1958 to urge the recovery of just-war discipline, said that this tradition had not been seriously respected and implemented for centuries:

---

[16] See Robert Rodes, "On Clandestine Warfare," *Washington and Lee Law Review* 39/2 (Spring 1982), 333-72.

[17] See Appendix IV below for the most important treaties.

The tendency to query the uses of the Catholic doctrine on war initially rises from the fact that it has for so long not been used, even by Catholics. That is, it has not been made the basis for a sound critique of public policies, and as a means for the formation of a right public opinion. The classic example, of course, was the policy of "unconditional surrender" during the last war. This policy clearly violated the requirement of the "right intention" that has always been a principle in the traditional doctrine of war. Yet no sustained criticism was made of the policy by Catholic spokesmen. Nor was any substantial effort made to clarify by moral judgment the thickening mood of savage violence that made possible the atrocities of Hiroshima and Nagasaki. I think it is true to say that the traditional doctrine was irrelevant during World War II. This is not an argument against the traditional doctrine. The Ten Commandments do not lose their imperative relevance by reason of the fact that they are violated.[18]

The theory was in the handbooks, but it was not stated trenchantly by theologians,[19] integrated in their instruction by the magisterium, preached by priests and chaplains, or respected by Catholic laity.

---

[18] "Theology and Modern War" in *Theological Studies* 20, (1959), pp. 40-61; previously an address to the Catholic Association for International Peace, subsequently reprinted in pamphlets and anthologies.

[19] The exceptions prove the rule. John Kenneth Ryan argued expertly that modern war by its nature cannot meet the requirements of last resort, just cause, or civilian immunity (*Modern War and Basic Ethics*, Ph.D. diss., Washington, D.C.: Catholic University of America, 1933; book edition Milwaukee: Bruce Press, 1940). John Ford, S.J., a decade later reviewed "The Morality of Obliteration Bombing" with a clear negative conclusion (*Theological Studies* [1944], 261-309).

CHAPTER 4

Hopes for Limiting War

Concurrent with the historic developments described in the previous chapter, and interlocking in complicated ways with them, some other changes took place that tended toward making restraint possible. None of these developments had quite the scale or effectiveness of the degenerative changes summarized above, to which they were partly a response, yet they were intrinsically valuable and provided some base for keeping alive the hope that Christian moral concern could exercise an effective, sobering influence.

The Cosmopolitan Vision

While Europe was breaking apart into a chaos of independent principalities and ultimately a score of nation-states, gradual progress in education and communication gave meaning, for a concerned minority, to the Renaissance vision of Europe as one humane community. Cosmopolitanism like that of Erasmus (d. 1536)[1] was the vision of only a few, but it retained high visibility and prestige as an alternative vision condemning the way things were going and proclaiming that they could be otherwise. In 1454 King George of Bohemia drew up the first of many peace

---

[1] Erasmus wrote several tracts against war, notably *A Complaint of Peace, War Is Sweet to the Uninformed* and *Institute of the Christian Prince* (see Bainton, *Christian Attitudes toward War and Peace*, 127-35).

plans to be projected by both thinkers and politicians. The Czech refugee educator Jan Amos Comenius (*Angel of Peace*, 1667), reformers such as William Penn (*Essay toward the Present and Future Peace of Europe*, 1693), philosophers like Immanuel Kant (*Perpetual Peace*, 1795), and authors like Victor Hugo (Address to Paris International Conference for Peace, 1849) projected visions of a European parliament possessing the moral power to mediate and arbitrate most conflicts and, if necessary, the military power to put down the rest.[2] Though never a reality (until 1919), this vision remained alive as a confession of impotence, and a morally powerful judgment on international anarchy, even though those who projected the critical vision were powerless to implement it.

Systematic Moral Theology and Law

The next development is best represented by the Dominican Francisco de Vitoria (d. 1546), writing in the face of the Iberian occupation of South America. Although by then the just-war tradition had been around for a millennium, it had remained only an implicit moral system, represented in the early fathers only by scattered fragments, in canon law only by occasional cases, and at the height of the Middle Ages only by a few paragraphs in the *Summa Theologica* of Thomas Aquinas.[3] Kings and generals paid little attention.

With Vitoria, for the first time we find an entire treatise[4] and the development of a full and coherent scholastic system of concepts able to address numerous issues in a way that is consistent from point to point and defended against alternative views. Since the Spanish and Portuguese presence in the New World was the nearest thing going on at that time to a holy war, Vitoria's clari-

---

[2] A listing of dozens of such projections through modern European history is available from the Joan B. Kroc Institute for International Peace Studies: *World Order Visions*; 7:WP:1, chapter 8.

[3] Aquinas, ST, II-II Q. 40, 41, 42.

[4] Francisco de Vitoria, *De Indis et de Iure Belli Relectiones*, in *Classics of International Law*, ed. J. Bates (Washington, D.C.: Carnegie Endowment for International Peace, 1944).

fication of the just-war tradition mattered practically. He progressively disentangled the justifiable war from the holy war and from the claim that it was proper for the empire to propagate the true religion. This disentanglement from the crusade type was also worked through on other grounds, less thoroughly, at about the same time, by the Protestant reformers, especially Martin Luther, but Vitoria's doing it within scholastic ethics, and in Spain, was to be of more abiding importance. A century later the Jesuit Francisco Suarez (d. 1617) went further[5] along the same path.

Responses to "Realism"

The move to disentangle the justifiable war from the crusade was roughly simultaneous with the argument against the naked "reason of state." Thanks to Machiavelli, moral thinkers could not avoid the challenge put to them by his cynical realism. In denouncing him and his moral relativism or opportunism, Christian thinkers restored, if not specifically the full just-war system, at least in a wider sense the concept that moral accountability applies also to princes.

Law of Nations

Thus far our topic has been the work of *ethicists*, that is, persons whose connection to the world of decision-making was only indirect, through the world of ideas, or through the ministry of the church. Their concepts, if respected at all, could only work in the minds of others who might solicit their counsel before a conflict or might respect their reprimands or absolution afterward.

Hugo Grotius (d. 1645) has become the symbolic representative of the next transition. The *law of nations* in the modern

---

[5] Francisco Suarez, Disputation 13 ("On Charity"), *The Three Theological Virtues*, trans. Williams, Brown, and Waldron, in Bates, *Classics of International Law*.

sense is usually dated from Grotius's first systematizing the tradition in *On the Law of War and Peace* (1625). The moral language used by the theologians was not difficult to translate into the language of the diplomat and the lawyer, so that the rules could serve as a basis for expert litigation and negotiation.[6] In this age diplomacy was becoming an orderly, expert profession. The increasing importance of sea travel, colonization, and piracy made imperative the creation of a legal system that most nations would have an interest in respecting and even in helping one another to enforce.

Grotius began his writings[7] as a philosopher and theologian, arguing (against the cynics and Machiavellians) that there is such a thing as moral obligation that cannot be attenuated in hard times, or suspended, and that such an obligation can and should be respected by leaders, even at some cost in terms of national interest. At the same time he argued against the pacifists (or even against the near-pacifist Erasmus), who saw no place at all for real war.

It was to be a long time before the network of legal insights and obligations that Grotius and other writers developed would become enforceable in some way other than the voluntary compliance of the rulers of Europe, within the terms of treaty agreements, but the foundation had been laid.[8] From this beginning could grow a body of tradition defining duties incumbent on sovereign nations in their dealings with one another, even though the question of enforcement became moot in the most important conflicts.

In the transition from the setting of morality to that of law, many elements of the classical thought pattern are easily trans-

---

[6] Grotius was himself a diplomat, serving various royal houses at different times. His was the age of the build-up to the Peace of Westphalia (1648), which inaugurated the vision of a Europe made up of sovereign but law-abiding and treaty-keeping states.

[7] The introductory chapter or "Prolegomena" in *On the Laws of War and Peace*, sometimes printed separately, makes his basic argument against what he calls "cynicism," something close to what we call realism.

[8] Many legal thinkers consider a law as real only if promulgated by a government that can enforce it. Yet much of international law does not have that sanction. More recently, nations have defined law by writing treaties with one another, but many of these treaties are not enforceable coercively.

lated. The dignity of the noncombatant is definable in both frames of reference, as is the notion of a righteous cause. Yet there are significant changes in the tone. A moral principle is generally stated with a view to the restraint it seeks to exercise or the good which should be performed. The law tends to be formulated in terms of how much it can permit or whether it will be able to inflict punishment. In law, prohibition is implemented by punishment or compensation. A hiatus arises in legal thought between what is sinful and what will be prosecuted, or between what is immoral and what the laws prohibit, and another between what the words of the law prohibit and what will in fact be enforced.[9] It becomes clear for a large part of the regulation of war that one reason one party can promise to keep the rules written into a treaty is that *if* the other party agrees and also keeps them, then both sides will gain by fighting fairly. This opens, or sharpens, some further questions:

1) What if the other party does not fight fairly? Are we then released from our obligation?[10]

2) Is the obligation based only on being ultimately in the selfish interests of both parties? Does it then cease to be binding, on the ground of "necessity,"[11] in the case where respecting the rules would become much more costly for one party than for the other?

3) Does the obligation defined by a treaty apply only to the parties who have signed the treaty? Or is it understood that the treaty only clarifies what was already a natural moral obligation binding on everyone?

4) Do the obligations defined in a treaty apply when the adversary is not a party to the treaty? Or can we declare that non-signatories are "beyond the pale"?

The end of the same period saw the development of international treaties following just-war concepts; this put into docu-

---

[9] One of the many legal themes we cannot pursue at length is the notion of a *dead letter*, that is, a rule that remains on the books but is enforced only selectively or not at all.

[10] We call this *reprisal*, and it has its own chapter in the just-war literature; e.g., see the references in the index of Walzer, *Just and Unjust Wars*.

[11] See the description above, pages 27f., of the ambivalence of the appeal to "necessity."

ments, to which states bound themselves contractually, the principles that previously had been mere imperatives in books written by diplomats like Grotius and teachers of law like Puffendorf or Vattel. Beginning with the Paris declaration on maritime law (1856) and the Red Cross convention on the wounded (Geneva 1864) the development continued with St. Petersburg on forbidden weapons, such as explosive projectiles (1868), culminating in a large collection of treaties signed at The Hague (1899, 1907).[12]

This development of treaties had begun within the spirit of the "concert of Europe," established after the fall of Napoleon. At first the thought was that the only parties bound to fight fairly according to these rules would be the parties who had signed them, so that they did not need to be respected when fighting against someone who was not committed to doing the same or who did not respect them.[13] Increasingly, however, the claim tended to gain ground that all nations, signatories or not, should respect the conventions, since they are mere clarifications and applications of general principles that were already valid for all before the treaties spelled them out.[14]

---

[12] A major stage was the Brussels treaty of 1874, but it was not ratified; basically the same provisions were picked up at The Hague. See Leon Friedman, *The Law of War, a Documentary History* (New York: Random House, 1972); Adam Roberts and Richard Guelff, eds., *Documents on the Laws of War* (New York: Oxford University Press, 1989); and John Sylvester Hemleben, *Plans for World Peace Through Six Centuries* (Chicago: University of Chicago Press, 1943).

[13] There can be more than one mode of nonapplicability: 1) The other party did not sign the treaties, so we need not respect them when fighting that party; thus the British in their war to restore control of South Africa did not need to respect the Boers, who had not existed as a nation when the treaties were signed. 2) We did not sign the treaties, so we are not bound to respect them; Japan had not signed those treaties dealing with the rights of prisoners, since they expected that no Japanese soldiers would be taken prisoners. So, when in World War II Japanese forces took prisoners, Japan was not bound by the Geneva conventions.

[14] This leaves open another question: How will the treaty provisions be implemented in domestic law? In the United States (*Constitution*, Article VI) a treaty as soon as ratified becomes the law of the land. Even that statement does not yet define how it will be implemented. In other legal systems the distance from signing a treaty to implementing its provisions may be longer.

Fitting the interest of the rulers of Europe, this network of treaty commitments began to move hesitantly toward a small approximation of the federalist vision.[15] Since then the slow progress in building institutions consistent with the just-war mentality has continued under the auspices of the League of Nations and the United Nations, although not as rapidly as the escalation of new threats.

Codes of Combat

It is yet another step when concern for restraining war advances from law texts to military procedure. The Middle Ages had manuals for the etiquette of knights and princes. It was assumed that the right to bear weapons was a privilege, which brought with it a special code of honor for how those weapons were to be used, especially with regard to the innocent. In the nineteenth century these codes began to be applied to the common soldier. They then could be enforced as a matter of military discipline. The codes stated in operational terms the obligations incumbent upon soldiers in the field.

It was especially imperative to think about these matters in the setting of the Civil War in the United States, since the "enemy" was one's own compatriots, fellow citizens the North wanted to hold within the same national community. Immigrant German jurist Francis Lieber was charged by the Secretary of War, at President Lincoln's request, with codifying what became "General Orders No. 100" (1863), often known as "Lieber's Code," the grandfather of modern military manuals.[16] From that point it became possible to hold a particular soldier or field office accountable for infringement of the rules of fair combat, truces, and safe conducts. The several U.S. armed services have their own manuals to aid field decision-makers in their respect for international law and to guide courtsmartial in sanctioning infractions.

---

[15] Most of the rules being defined applied only to *jus in bello*; the sweeping assumption of national sovereignty provided no way to define limits *ad bellum*.
[16] In Friedman, *The Law of War*, 158ff.

Regaining Intellectual Control of the Agenda

The Holy See

The "total" wars of Napoleonic Europe and the American Civil War crossed new thresholds in destructiveness. Some of the Great Powers' adventures in Asia demonstrated blatant governmental disregard for the laws of war.[17] This degeneration triggered a first critical response from the Roman Catholic bishops in their capacity as moral shepherds in the West.[18] Modern war has become indiscriminate in its targeting, disproportionate in scale, and governments have become unaccountable. The ecumenical council convened at the Vatican in 1870 had on its agenda proposals to declare that modern warfare must be brought under control by the creation of a Vatican office that would research and evaluate each proposed war with a view to measuring its legitimacy.[19]

The first Roman Catholic ecumenical council in modern times never got to this question for two reasons. First, it had to concentrate on the definition of papal infallibility. Second, it had to break up prematurely because of the outbreak of the Franco-Prussian war, which led to the invasion of the Vatican State. Nonetheless, this episode counts as a positive testimony to the value and objectivity of the doctrine. In the agenda preparation there was serious consideration by the bishops of the *notion* that the tradition *might* be more stringently applied, as an exercise of the pastoral responsibility of the magisterium. It is important that this awareness arose well before Hiroshima.

---

[17] Diplomat David Urquhart, a primary intellectual leader in this movement, was first sensitized to these issues when in 1839 Britain invaded both China and Afghanistan without the knowledge of Parliament or even the authorization of the cabinet. My study "David Urquhart and the Challenge of 'Just War' at Vatican I" is available on request from the Joan B. Kroc Institute for International Peace Studies, Notre Dame, IN 46556 (document 3:WP:8).

[18] See John Howard Yoder, *Nevertheless: The Varieties and Shortcomings of Religious Pacifism*, 2d ed. (Scottdale, Penn.: Herald Press, 1992), 15ff., 38ff. In this work I show how a strong antiwar concern can be more pastoral than pacifist, especially on the part of hierarchies. This was already the case for Pius IX, and even more for Benedict XV.

[19] See Yoder, "David Urquhart and the Challenge of 'Just War' at Vatican I."

Political Objectivity in One Nation

Berlin University pastor Franciscus Stratmann supported his own government at the beginning of World War I but came to a position of honest dissent before 1918. From then until his death in 1971 Stratmann remained the primary European Catholic spokesman for the unacceptability of modern war according to Catholic teaching. He was removed from his campus pastorate in 1917 but was never formally silenced by the Catholic episcopacy.

Papal Peace Statements

Beginning with Benedict XV during World War I, we find this *moral* insight—that modern war is overstepping just-war restraints—being increasingly transposed into the pastoral teaching of the popes. Benedict was powerless to keep the Catholics of Germany and those of France from proclaiming on each side that their war was just, but at least he could call war a scourge, intervene diplomatically to humanize it a little (e.g., calling for the humane treatment of prisoners), and could preach about the imperative of peace in the future. He inaugurated the pattern, which Pius XII was to renew during World War II, of addressing a message to the world every Christmas that centered on an appeal to peace, derived from the best vision of the just-war tradition.

Never, however, either in the First World War or the Second, did a pope intervene to tell the faithful in any one country that their war was unjust, as the tradition theoretically would have called on him to do. Nonetheless, the existence of the pope, as a symbol of the transnational unity of the Christian church according to the Roman Catholic self-understanding, kept the issue of the moral justification of international hostilities more alive in the minds of Catholics than it was for many Protestants.

Catholic Moral Theology in the Face of City Bombing

To that abiding sense of supranational community was added something of the intellectual rigor of Catholic thought, so the next step in making the just-war tradition concrete was also taken by Catholics. John C. Ford's review of "The Morality of Obliteration Bombing" is widely referred to as a landmark in the debate about the legitimacy of the massive aerial bombing of cities in World War II. The status, courage, and visibility of Professor Ford called attention to his article, although his statement was not the first. In fact, most of what he published in 1944 had been written in 1933 in a Catholic University of America doctoral thesis by John Kenneth Ryan.[20]

The argument of Ryan and Ford is simple and, on the level of straight logic, incontrovertible. The last years of World War I had made it clear that in the next war there would be aerial bombing of cities. In the course of disarmament negotiations up through 1933, the awareness of how destructive this would be and how hard to control had grown. Ryan had all the information needed to see the scale of the new moral problem.[21]

Even if, under the impact of the notion of total war, we have to grant that *some* of the people on the other side who are not soldiers are nonetheless in some sense enemies,[22] that can never be true for *everyone*. There are still great numbers of the civilian population in cities under the enemy's control who continue to belong in the category of innocent. There is no moral justification for tactics of warfare that threaten or take the lives of these people.

Ryan, followed by Ford, also reviewed the traditional Catholic logic of *double effect*, whereby it is considered permissible to do deeds that one recognizes to be in some sense "materially evil" (i.e., they harm someone), at the same time that one can hold them to be justified by virtue of other (good) effects that they seek and obtain. Ryan and Ford did not set this argument aside as morally unworthy, as many critics of casuistry from

---

[20] Ryan, *Modern War and Basic Ethics*.

[21] It was also being presented theoretically by the strategic theorist Douhet, who was in favor of maximal destruction from the air as the way to end a war quickly.

[22] This can be argued either on the grounds of their economic contribution, i.e., the notion of the "quasi-combatant work force," or because they are in moral solidarity with the cause of the war. Either of these conditions weakens the classical meaning of innocence.

Pascal to the present have done, nor did they seek to transpose it into a theoretically more refined proportionalism, as some Catholics in our day do. They assumed its legitimacy as a possible argument, but demonstrated carefully that it cannot apply to the kind of case and the scale of destruction that city bombing entails.

American Catholics seem not to have taken the Ryan/Ford argument seriously before Hiroshima. In Britain, on the other hand, the debate about city bombing was public and intense. Journalist George Orwell was one of the strong voices against letting just-war limits forbid killing civilians.[23] On the other side there were some bishops who made an issue of the matter in the House of Lords,[24] and there were some pacifists who used just-war categories in the hope of convincing nonpacifists.

There were differences between the Royal Air Force, whose General Arthur Harris favored obliteration bombing, and the United States Air Force, whose General Arnold was more committed to trying to respect the traditional disciplines of discrimination in targeting.[25]

In all of this renewal of just-war awareness the focus was on only one of the many classical criteria, namely, the immunity of noncombatant personnel. This one criterion was sufficiently powerful to eliminate one particular kind of strategy, namely, the worst one. No one thought to challenge the claim that innocent immunity was traditionally imperative. Those who chose not to respect its limits recognized that they were choosing not to be bound by the constraints of the tradition. They most easily claimed the ground of military necessity, which was held to be extreme in this circumstance because of the dramatic dimensions of the Nazi threat. If Hitler truly threatened the survival of the

---

[23] George Orwell, "As I Please," *The Collected Essays of George Orwell*, vol. 3 (London: Secker & Warburg, 1968), 199-252.

[24] See *The Collected Essays of George Orwell*, vol. 3, 151-52; Walzer, *Just and Unjust Wars*, 262. Orwell argued that the notion of civilian immunity was "one of the things that made war possible." An example of the debate in the House of Lords between a bishop and a viscount is recorded in Albert Marrin, ed., *War and the Christian Conscience* (Chicago: Regnery Press, 1971), 147-54.

[25] Stephen A. Garrett, *Ethics and Airpower in World War II: The British Bombing of German Cities* (New York: St. Martin's Press, 1993).

entire system of Western freedoms, one should not have to respect *all* the rules when combatting him. If one could end a war more quickly by not keeping all of the rules, the total cost of winning by breaking them might be less than dragging out the war by respecting the rules.[26]

The Nuclear Hurdle

As we noted concerning the bishops in 1870, the bishops and Stratmann during World War I, and Ryan and Ford in World War II, the above-stated condemnation of area bombing was formulated well before the conscience of the world was shaken by the step across the nuclear threshold. Nevertheless, it was that step which convinced a far greater public that there must be a stopping point.

One can debate whether the atomic threshold is crucial in every respect. The total damage done to lives and properties at Hiroshima was not in every way disproportionate to the earlier conventional bombings of Hamburg, Dresden, and Tokyo.[27] Nonetheless, a psychological threshold had been crossed, even if in the future it would be whittled down to look more as if there were a gradual continuum from conventional to tactical nuclear levels of destruction.

To the question of immunity—particular categories of people who ought not to be destroyed—the full-fledged development of city bombing, especially if nuclear, added very clearly the question of proportionality, that is, the quantitative measure of the total amount of damage done compared to the damage done (or intended) by the other side. How "proportionality" was to be measured is something the older traditions were never very clear

---

[26] Walzer spells out the argument for a notion of "supreme emergency" that would authorize breaking the rules "just this once" while still claiming to honor them otherwise. See Walzer, *Just and Unjust Wars*, 245-55, 261, 267f., 274, 323, 327.

[27] Part of the disproportion was the additional dimensions of radiation and worldwide fallout, not all of which were known about at the time. More people were killed in those other cities, and to die in a burning city may be slower and more painful.

about, but the enormous escalation of destructive potential makes any rational person ask whether there must not be a limit *somewhere*, such that to go beyond it would be too much. It makes a logical difference, but hardly a moral one, whether the nuclear threshold is identified as immunity, proportion, or discrimination. William V. O'Brien noted that recent papal statements accentuate being "indiscriminate" as what is unacceptable; he asks whether they refer to immunity or to proportion.[28] The logical answer is that both are implied; control of the impact of one's means is the precondition of respecting any kind of restraint. Thus to be uncontrollable is a vice in its own right. Even before a use actually occurs which is illegitimate on grounds of immunity or proportion, the creation of an instrument that is by its very nature uncontrollable is illegitimate.

Such a limit was first stated by military scientist Commander Sir Stephen King-Hall of the British Royal Navy. Just a week after Hiroshima he wrote in his professional newsletter that the development of this new category of weaponry had to put an end to the possibility of full-scale war between major powers on purely technical military grounds. He expanded his argument into a book, *Defense in a Nuclear Age*,[29] initiating a line of military thinkers who reject current military strategies on the grounds of tactical/technical military feasibility, as well as on just-war moral and legal grounds.[30]

It is this notion that there must be a limit somewhere which in the 1950s came to be called *nuclear pacifism*, even though in its logic it is a form of just-war thinking. It is generally not linked with firm quantitative argument about just where that limit is, but those who hold to it are convinced that an all-out nuclear exchange, or, of course, an all-out nuclear strike against an enemy population center, would be illicit.

Such a limit was stated by a study commission convened by the World Council of Churches (a world body which at that

---

[28] William V. O'Brien, *Christian Ethics and Nuclear War* (Washington, D.C.: Georgetown University Press, 1961).

[29] Sir Stephen King-Hall, *Defense in a Nuclear Age* (London: Gollancz, 1958; New York: Fellowship Publications, 1959).

[30] Strictly speaking, military and moral grounds cannot be separated. Probable success is one of the criteria of the just-war tradition.

time linked most major Protestant and Greek Orthodox bodies) under the heading *Christians and the Prevention of War in a Nuclear Age* (1957) and in similar ways by Pope John XXIII in his encyclical *Peace on Earth* (1963). Theologians John C. Murray, Paul Ramsey, and Helmut Gollwitzer were among the first of many voices saying the same thing. Bryan Hehir wrote that "a strong and solid consensus has formed against any use of nuclear weapons however limited."[31] He said this, however, in the context of a report which went on to add that secular political thinkers were moving away from rather than toward that consensus, seeking to widen the room for some exceptionally acceptable usage of nuclear arms.[32] Meanwhile, careful just-war thinkers who reject that expansion are logically just like pacifists in that they take positions on fundamental moral grounds without the certainty that they could be implemented successfully, and without the assent of the people who make the political choices.

Nuremberg

Even before the successful conclusion of World War II, the allies had decided not only that they would claim the rights of victors to reorder the postwar world, but that they would punish the persons guilty of crimes committed in the prosecution of the war. We may use the name *Nuremberg* as our code term for the series of war-crimes tribunals, the first, largest, and most publicized of which were held in that German city.[33] Crimes

---

[31] Bryan Hehir, *Commonweal* (March 13, 1981).

[32] The term *use* is deceptive. Threatening is also use. Not only was there for decades the maximum reciprocal threat between the superpowers, but lesser countries were also threatened. A mugger *uses* his pistol when he points it at my head, even if he does not fire. The United States has used its nuclear potential as a threat more than once (see Daniel Ellsberg, "Introduction," *Protest and Survive*, ed. E. P. Thompson and Dan Smith [New York: Monthly Review Press, 1981]). In the same sense, the threats made to Tarik Aziz and Saddam Hussein of Iraq by Secretary Baker and President Bush, to the effect that if Iraq used nuclear weapons the United States would retaliate, constituted use.

[33] Other trials were held in various places in Europe and Asia. The Pacific theater also had similar trials. These, however, were less persuasive, as the Indian judge dissented on the grounds that ex post facto prosecution was unfair.

against "the laws of war," "peace," and "humanity" were prosecuted.

Discussion continues as to the legal and moral dimensions of
the Nuremberg prosecution. This justice was imposed by the victors on the vanquished. An impressively careful procedure was
established, whereby judges from the four Allied nations tried
the accused according to the safeguards of both the Anglo-Saxon
and the Napoleonic legal traditions. Some consider the fact that
this was "victor's justice"—and the fact that Allied infractions
were not punished—to be automatically unfair. Yet it can be argued that that is true of all legal conflict. Every court represents
a power structure that some time in the past has put down its
opponents. Every court's decision to punish is selective.

There were important discrepancies among the several legal
traditions of the victorious allies represented at Nuremberg regarding how they explained the court's jurisdiction and how they
defined the crimes to be punished. Some are critical on the
grounds of the Anglo-Saxon rejection of ex post facto laws (punishing deeds which were not identified as crimes when they were
committed).[34] Nonetheless, the trials provided institutional dem-
onstration for the claim that it is morally and legally incumbent
on persons other than sovereigns to refuse to obey an unjust
order.[35]

Nuremberg showed, by acting it out on a stage the whole world
could watch, that one may be prosecuted later for having failed
to disobey an unjust order. It thereby constitutes a symbolic statement by the victors, in that the distinction they make between
those losers whom they prosecute and those who are not prosecuted is based upon the classical laws of war. That Nuremberg
through due process exonerated some people (thereby protect-
ing them from blind retaliation) is just as important for the rule
of law as the fact that it condemned some. Thus the basic no-

---

[34] Genocide, the deliberate elimination of a people on racial grounds, had
not until then been listed on the books as a crime. The prosecution claimed that
even if not previously written down in those words, those rules were rooted in
already universally known principles of natural law.

[35] The Nuremberg rules conceded that having committed a crime "under orders" might mitigate the severity of the punishment, but it was never a grounds
for exoneration from guilt.

tions of just-war legality were reinforced, even though the prospect of such enforcement after a war would hardly function powerfully to restrain anyone otherwise inclined to commit a war crime in the interest of increasing his chances of winning or in the prosecution of an ideological war where cost is no consideration.[36]

The trials at Nuremberg were thus not a wasted effort. They were soon to be appealed to by a few political scientists and lawyers in the American Vietnam debate, as having established legal precedent, within the American system, for persons whose disobedience to the draft was based upon the conviction that the service asked of them would be illegal.[37]

The Morally Responsible Citizen Draftee

We observed that war had become "total" by involving whole populations in its destruction, both as victims and as perpetrators. Now we turn to another dimension of modernity, namely, the idea of citizen responsibility. Ancient and medieval thought, when the just-war tradition was born and grew, had little concept of the citizen as an independent and responsible moral actor. Theologians around 1200 had said that a vassal was not obligated to aid his lord in an unjust war, but they did not declare it to be his duty to refuse to serve. The prince, not the vassal, was to blame for any injustice. It has been logically possible since the Reformation for a soldier or citizen to conclude that a given war was unjustified and therefore to choose to refuse to serve, yet such a development was unlikely. Martin Luther had written that *if* a soldier knew his lord was fighting for an unjust cause, it was the soldier's responsibility to refuse

---

[36] In April 1995 a tribunal at The Hague set up by the United Nations began naming the Serbian leaders accused of war crimes against Bosnian civilians. Some regretted the announcement, fearing that it would only lengthen the war.

[37] See Telford Taylor, *Nuremberg and Vietnam: An American Tragedy* (Chicago: Quadrangle Books, 1970). Taylor had been the Chief Counsel for the United States at Nuremberg, which made his view of the parallel especially weighty. American courts have not accepted the argument as justifying civil disobedience in the United States.

to serve, even at the cost of his life, but very few conscientious Lutherans over the centuries made use of this logical possibility.[38] In the most recent dramatic experience in Luther's homeland, even persons who opposed the Nazi regime in principle still accepted military service.[39]

The logical necessity of refusing to serve in an unjust war finally broke through on an impressive scale in the American Vietnam experience. Thousands of young men refused to serve for reasons derived not from absolutist pacifism but from their own conscientious, although not always articulate, application of the just-war criteria. They thought the Vietnam hostilities lacked legitimate authority because of their opinion of the South Vietnamese regime or because the presence of American soldiers in combat overseas was not authorized by a formal declaration of war. They considered the means to be improper because of what they heard about civilian casualties, free-fire zones, napalm, and defoliation. They considered the cause to be questionable because they gave some credence to the American national vision according to which government is legitimate only with the consent of the governed, so that the preservation of a dictatorial regime in Saigon, or preventing third-world peoples from choosing socialism, were not valid purposes for which to fight. Proportionality was questionable, and so was probable success, the longer the war wore on.

Some of these young men believed the public rhetoric, according to which the war was not about the welfare of the citizens of Vietnam but rather was a global conflict between America as center of "the free world" and communist imperialism on the other side, with Vietnam simply the turf on which that global

---

[38] During the Vietnam War, American Lutheran church agencies, like Roman Catholic ones, affirmed the possibility of "selective objection."

[39] German theologians Helmut Gollwitzer and Jurgen Moltmann, although rejecting the Nazi cause, both accepted military service and finished the war as prisoners of war. The most striking (and very rare) case of a person who did reject military service on just-war grounds was the Austrian Catholic Franz Jagerstatter (see Gordon Zahn, *In Solitary Witness: The Life and Death of Franz Jägerstatter* (Springfield, Ill.: Templegate Publishers, 1986).

battle was being fought.[40] Such applications of the just-war criteria were far more convincing to the average American citizen, whether draftee or voter, than the more demanding traditional pacifist appeals would have been.

No way was found for the selective service system to respond fairly to this new phenomenon.[41] Yet this stance, which came to be called *selective conscientious objection*, came in the 1970s to be recognized as a valid moral option by leaders of the major church bodies.[42] The fact that a Quaker or Amish young man, rejecting all wars as his church teaches, could be recognized as a conscientious objector and given alternative service, whereas a Catholic or Lutheran draftee, evaluating wars case by case as his church teaches, could not, represents a kind of backhanded establishment of religion.

---

[40] A strong early statement of the negative just-war reading on Vietnam was Philip Wogaman, "A Moral Assessment of the War in Vietnam," *Christian Century* (January 4, 1967).

[41] From the governmental perspective, just-war dissent based on the facts of the case rather than on some inner conscience appears to be no more than glorifying theologically one's political views.

[42] A collection of statements on "The Moral Duty to Refuse to Serve in an Unjust War" is available from the Joan B. Kroc Institute for International Peace Studies, Notre Dame, IN 46556 (document 3:WP:9).

CHAPTER 5

The Tradition and the Real World

As we near the end of the conversation with the just-war tradition, we can tie a few threads together. The following observations about the terrain we have covered will not constitute a final judgment on the validity of the just-war tradition, but they may help the reader to test some preliminary experience-based conclusions about its status as classical consensus.

The Scale Keeps Sliding

The reader will already be aware that the just-war tradition as a whole is more complicated than it sounded at first. It has numerous necessary sub-themes, and its terms presuppose prior definitions, many of them debatable, without which the system cannot work. More important, though, its fundamental logic is ambivalent. The just-war tradition says that war is generally deplorable and is always in need of being limited—and that there are ways to limit it. These ways, it is held, are relevant and effective, so that those who (regretfully) have recourse to lethal violence can be assured that what they are doing is not murder.

The credibility of this statement, morally and logically, is tied to the degree to which the defined criteria actually impose effective restraints. Beneath the basic concession—that some exceptions will have to be made to the general rule of the wrongness of killing—we come upon a still "lower" level of exceptions to the need for exceptional justifications. The different arguments

50

to which we now turn will be seen to carry different weights for different persons, and they proceed on different levels. Yet their cumulative impact is to decrease the credibility of the tradition and the applicability of the limits initially stated.

Lowering the Hurdles

Any set of rules, obviously, will tend to favor the interests of those who wrote it. As technology changes, rules will be written to favor those parties whose strength was greatest in terms of the older technology.[1] Two examples are obvious in recent strategic history.

a) The earlier rules defined those who have the right to be considered soldiers (rather than as bandits or common criminals) by their wearing a uniform (or other visible, distinguishing sign) and carrying their arms in the open. Modern times have seen an escalation of the importance of irregular or guerrilla forces (called terrorists by their enemies and freedom fighters by their friends), whose operation would be rendered impossible by obeying those earlier rules. So we need new rules, which permit guerrilla war, in order to regulate it. United Nations negotiations since 1949 have begun to make such changes.[2]

b) The earlier rules for submarine warfare, derived from those for surface naval combat, forbade torpedoing a ship without confirming that it was in fact armed. To do that, the submarine would have to surface, which made it vulnerable, sacrificing the entire advantage of being a submarine, especially in the face of the British ruse of secretly arming what looked like merchant

---

[1] This is argued with special force in Chris af Jochnick and Roger Norman, "Legitimation of Violence: A Critical History of the Laws of War," *Harvard International Law Review* 35 (1994): 49-85; and Jochnick and Norman, "The Legitimation of Violence: A Critical Analysis of the Gulf War," *Harvard International Law Review* 35 (1994): 387ff.

[2] Increasing numbers of younger nations, now represented in the United Nations commissions which rewrite the rules, look back to origins in irregular warfare. Robert E. Rodes, Jr., proposes an updated body of *in bello* law to make fighting fair possible in such circumstances ("On Clandestine Warfare," *Washington and Lee Law Review* 39/2 [Spring 1982], 333-72). There is parallel material in Michael Howard, *Restraints on War* (New York: Oxford University Press, 1979), 33ff. and 135ff.

vessels. It was thus no surprise that the Germans disregarded this rule during World War II.

The victorious Allies, stronger on the surface and weaker undersea, reaffirmed the old rules in new treaties written in the 1920s, but they were again disregarded in World War II *on both sides*. In the Nuremberg trials Allied submarine commanders testified in defense of German commanders accused of ignoring these rules, saying that Allied submarines had disregarded them too.[3]

These two examples illustrate the principle that rules are more likely to be kept if they are less demanding and more realistic. One therefore consents to sacrifice one part of the values which the original rules safeguarded in the hope of avoiding complete lawlessness. In the interest of maintaining restraint in a minimal way, one agrees to relax the particular restraints that would really have made it more difficult to continue hostilities and to win. It is thought better to have a few modest rules that both sides can afford to keep rather than more demanding requirements that will not be respected.

Going farther in this same direction, William V. O'Brien has argued that the principle of noncombatant immunity can no longer be effectively respected.[4] Instead of continuing to affirm it abstractly but undercutting its meaning by the use of arguments of necessity and double effect, it would be more appropriate to declare it a dead letter and to concentrate on building up those other restraints that are still realistic.

As we already noted briefly, George Orwell, the British journalist better known for the novels *Animal Farm* and *1984*, was

---

[3] The literature is strikingly devoid of attention to the phenomenon of the "dead letter," i.e., a law all parties tacitly agree need not be obeyed and infractions of which will not be punished. During World War II, that is what submarine commanders on both sides thought of these rules, and the tribunal agreed.

[4] William V. O'Brien, *War and/or Survival* (Garden City: Doubleday, 1969), 248ff. He argues that to insist firmly on noncombatant immunity is tantamount to pacifism. While constantly restated as an ideal, noncombatant immunity has been losing ground since Napoleon. To be honest in the nuclear age, we should drop that hurdle. Later, O'Brien argues further that noncombatant immunity cannot be and has never been respected, because by definition discrimination is contradictory to self-defense (*The Conduct of Just and Limited War* [New York: Praeger Publishers 1981], 44ff.). This is certainly an exaggeration.

saying something similar during World War II. Once one has resolved to accept war at all, it is better to get it over with quickly, by whatever means, rather than let it be strung out and the total destructiveness increased by placing artificial limits on the use of one's best weapons. When the enemy's troops are draftees, they may be morally just as innocent as the aged. Why should a war be better which kills only healthy young people?[5]

Necessity

The classic just-war tradition said that the means used in war should be "necessary and proportionate." That rejected wanton or vengeful destruction and any damage not directly functional toward the goal of winning the war. Necessity was thus a supplemental criterion operative *within* the limits set by the other rules. It was classically so defined by Francis Lieber in 1863,[6] and it was so defined in the U.S. Army Field Manual 27-10 of 1956:

> The prohibitory effect of the law of war is not minimized by "military necessity" which has been defined as that principle which justifies *those measures not forbidden* by international law which are indispensable for securing the complete submission of the enemy as soon as possible. Military necessity has been generally rejected as a defense for acts forbidden by the customary and conventional laws of war (inasmuch as the latter have been developed and framed with consideration for the concept of military necessity).

Yet increasingly the ordinary use of necessity in the popular mind has become the opposite. It has come to mean a claimed justification for breaking one or another of the rules if one "really has to." "Really having to" depends, of course, on a judgment concerning the particular value that is at stake at the time. It may mean a captain's not wanting to jeopardize his troop's lives "unnecessarily"; a general not wanting to risk the outcome

---

[5] George Orwell, "As I Please."
[6] See Lieber, "General Orders No. 100" (1863), in Friedman, 158-85.

of a particular battle; or a statesman not wanting to prolong, or to lose, "unnecessarily," a war.

The practical effect of this shift is to reduce necessity to utility, providing *carte blanche* for any destruction that is not purely wanton, wasteful, or vengeful.[7] Yet this fact is not openly avowed; phrases like "only if it is *really* necessary" preserve the illusion that there is still a limit. One claims not to have descended to the level where "anything goes."

Political philosopher Michael Walzer, whose *Just and Unjust Wars* has done much to enhance the seriousness of discourse in this field, has proposed a yet more complex version of the necessity argument, namely, the notion of *supreme emergency*, which authorizes overriding the normal restraints of law and morality, but only if in fact all of civilization is at stake. How does one measure that? Taking off from the ancient maxim, Let justice be done even if the heavens fall, Walzer claims justification for an exception, "*but only if the heavens are (really) about to fall*" (emphasis added).[8]

They Did It First

This theme also characterizes a long spectrum of degrees of infraction. The minimum is a specific act of reprisal overtly identified as a breach of the usual rules and as intended to punish the adversary for an infraction and prevent its recurrence.[9] This calls for a renewed application, on the new lower level, of the notions of proportion and discrimination. There needs to be a way to communicate with enemies (for example, through the Red Cross) so that they know:

- that we will do to them what they do to us;
- that the act is not a gratuitous escalation but a targeted reprisal, from which it follows

---

[7] See Wasserstrom, "The Laws of War" and Taylor, "War Crimes," in Wakin, *War, Morality, and the Military Profession*, 2d ed. (Boulder, Col.: Westview, 1986), 394ff., 400ff., 375ff.; and Walzer, *Just and Unjust Wars*, 254, 144ff.

[8] Walzer, *Just and Unjust Wars*, 230-31. How one determines this Walzer does not say. Since the heavens' falling is a metaphor, there is no simple explanation of what "(really)" means.

[9] Ibid., 207ff.

• that we will stop doing it if they do.

Thus the (stated) intention of the single infraction is to restore respect for the rules; the retaliatory infringement must go no farther than the original offense did.

A more sweeping loosening of the rules results if one gives more weight to the dimension of contract thinking that obtained in the development of the international conventions. What those treaties forbid, in detail, is not wrong primarily morally or intrinsically. Its wrongness is defined by the treaty, conventionally, because two parties, in the interest of both, have agreed to fight fairly, and that fairness is defined by those rules. If, however, the other side breaks the rules, "the deal is off" and we are no longer bound by them either. If they have made military use of vehicles marked with a red cross, the immunity of the wounded has thereby been sacrificed.[10] We claim that we are still more moral than they, but we descend to fight them on their terms.

They Are Unworthy

The identity of the adversaries whose rights the just-war tradition protects is not fully clear in the tradition. On the one hand, it would seem natural that since all the values we talk about needing to respect are those of our enemies, it would hardly be fitting to distinguish between those enemies to whom we do and those to whom we do not owe such restraint. Yet as the tradition evolved and was applied, there often has been such differentiation, denying that *all* adversaries have the same rights. This fact should be no surprise. Just-war standards are then thought of as something like the good manners that should exist among the citizens of civil society. Warfare that respects the rules is then something like a court trial or a duel. The medieval limitations against illicit weapons or tactics forbade their use only against Christians, assuming that against the infidel the standards could be lower. Thus the conceptual wedge between the just war, properly so-called, and the holy war alternative begins to exist as a

---

[10] In the 1991 Gulf War allied military spokesmen claimed that the killing of civilians in Baghdad was justified by the fact that Saddam Hussein should not have permitted civilians to take shelter in buildings the allies considered military targets.

wedge between two kinds of adversaries as well. The infidel (or the barbarian), being beyond the pale of civility, did not possess even those rights the just-war tradition protected.

In modern times the notion remains that adversaries can put themselves "beyond the pale" and forfeit their right to be fought against fairly. Sometimes this can be argued on the grounds that the adversary was not a party to the treaty that defined the rules. The Afrikaner nations that faced the British in the Boer war had claimed independence for years, but they had not been represented at the drafting of The Hague conventions; so the British, fighting to force them back into the Empire, could claim that they did not count as a legitimate war-making authority. Thus the British could treat them as common brigands. The British developed new inhumane forms of conflict—the concentration camp and scorched earth—partly under the pretext that the enemy did not exist as a people. A parallel argument has raged more recently in Northern Ireland, Algeria, Latin America, and South Africa over whether insurrectionists when captured should be treated as political prisoners or as common criminals.

Before 1939 Japan had not signed some of the international conventions on the treatment of prisoners of war, partly because of the conviction that Japanese soldiers would not be taken prisoner. Thus it could not be demanded of Japan with force of law that Allied prisoners of war in the Asian theater during World War II be cared for under those rules.

Perhaps more often, one or more of the parties are declared to be "beyond the pale" not because of a document they did not sign, but because they broke the rule first, and thereby qualified themselves as outlaws rather than as combatants. The right to be fought against according to the laws of war would then, the argument goes, be revocable.

The escalation of the evil we allow ourselves to commit on the ground of the special evil incarnate in the adversary has often seemed convincing, especially when exacerbated by ideological and/or racial overtones. The Turks had that image in the late Middle Ages (and still do for Armenians and Greeks), Nazism had it in the mid-twentieth century, and communism had it until recently.

Though generally critical of what he called the logic of the "sliding scale," Michael Walzer was open, as we saw, to arguing for a specific "supreme emergency" in favor of the massive bombing of German cities, because a Nazi victory—qualitatively different from most losses in most wars—would have meant the end of certain basic values of world civilization.[11] I mentioned this before as a special form of the necessity argument, but for it to be convincing one must have made some previous global judgments about Nazism and civilization.

Here again we observe a shift from intrinsic morality to contract thinking. According to this notion we are not obligated to honor the dignity of the enemy noncombatant population because they are human, but only because their government has made and keeps a commitment to carry on the combat according to our rules. If their rulers deny our basic value system, the enemies (not only the rulers but the populations) forfeit the privilege of our respect. It was, in sum, a privilege that we, being morally superior, had bestowed upon them. Or it was a conditional right they had earned by meeting us on our terrain, rather than an intrinsic right by virtue of their humanity. "Savages" and "outlaws" have no intrinsic rights.[12] Thus the worse the enemy's cause, the more room we may have to break the rules.

Situationism

Many of the common-sense responses that arise in the effort to move just-war thought beyond the first phases of superficial realism take the shape of anti-intellectual or antistructural reasoning. "In a combat situation there is not time for complicated calculation of possibilities."[13] "When the lives of my men are at

---

[11] Walzer, *Just and Unjust Wars*, 253ff.

[12] Soon after the bombing of Hiroshima, President Truman made much of the fact that Japan had treacherously attacked Pearl Harbor and had not treated war prisoners humanely. Both accusations were true, but neither of those crimes was committed by the people of Hiroshima, and neither of them suspended the adhesion of the United States to The Hague treaties, which forbade that kind of attack. Truman's first announcements had in fact claimed that Hiroshima was a military base.

[13] Sometimes in the ethical parlance of the last two generations "situation ethics" meant simply that one must take account of every element of a setting to be able to decide morally. Here it may mean a stronger case: "The heat of battle" may count as a reason to be less careful.

stake, philosophy is not very convincing." The normal penchant of the selfish heart and the lazy mind for such excuses is precisely why we need to have rules and to think about them before the crisis.[14] It is precisely because there is little time and the stakes may be great that decision-makers need reminders of the fundamental rights of other parties in the conflict, rights which remain binding even in the midst of unavoidable conflict. Precisely because abstract analysis is not easy under fire, the limits of our entitlement to destroy our fellow humans' lives and property need to be formulated and rehearsed ahead of time, to protect ourselves as well as others against our (partially, but not infinitely) justified self-interest.

Systematizing Moral Thought

Whereas some of the least morally worthy adjustments, like those just described, use ordinary debating language, or even anti-academic "realism" appeals, and whereas some of them claim the superior authority of the lay person against the more complex work of the specialist, there is one line of argument which claims deep roots in the tradition of moral theologians. The doctrine of double effect claims a long history, offering to throw light on especially difficult choices in which competing or coinciding values cannot be separated from one another, so that in order to ward off one evil it seems that one must accept another. Thus the case one makes for needing to break one rule can be interpreted as part of a larger rule-governed process of adjudication.

Moral theologians are far from agreeing on the precise interpretation and justification of this pattern of argument, but there is agreement on its basic outlines.[15] One must be able to show that:

a) The evil which happens (the secondary effect of the action) is less than the evil which is prevented;

---

[14] John Courtney Murray, S.J., "Remarks on the Moral Problem of War," *Theological Studies* 20 (1959), 40-61.

[15] A landmark treatment of the theme is *Doing Evil to Achieve Good*, ed. Richard C. McCormick, S.J., and Paul Ramsey (Chicago: Loyola University Press, 1978). Walzer also reviews the theme (*Just and Unjust Wars*, 152-59).

b) The evil which happens, though it is the outcome of the entire set of situations and events, is not itself the actual cause of the good results (or one would be directly doing evil for the sake of good, which is not permitted);

c) The evil which happens is not willed or intended;

d) The actual deed, which both triggers the unintended evil byproduct and is indispensable to the primary intended good, is not in itself intrinsically wrong.

It cannot be our agenda here to review the appropriateness of double-effect reasoning as a whole, as a mode of moral argument.[16] I note only that it constitutes a powerful intellectual apparatus contributing to the downward drift, while still claiming to hold the line somewhere. Some argue that the just-war theory as a whole represents a case of double-effect reasoning, where the killing of enemies is the regrettable and unintended result of the intrinsically good defense of national values. Others, however, would use double-effect argument on the next lower level: the evil one regretfully accepts for the sake of a higher good is not the killing itself, or war itself, but the fact that one pursues one's war goals in infraction of one or another of the just-war criteria.[17] Thus one can discuss, for instance, the acceptance of noncombatant casualties or the misuse of Red Cross protection, as a lesser evil, not intended but regretfully accepted as a part of the price for a higher good. It is not easy for the critic who wants to be fair to know where the line runs between careful casuistic good faith and plain cynical abuse.

This Far and No Farther?

The earliest firm landmark in the development of what came to be called nuclear pacifism was a study process convened by the Study Department of the World Council of Churches follow-

---

[16]Some would argue that all four criteria can be redefined as proportional reasoning about the values at stake in a decision. Critics of the system challenge the definitions of each of the terms. Can one deny intending the foreseeable results of one's acts? Does the intrinsic-evil category include anything that it would be costly to renounce doing?

[17]This is what Walzer assumes when he digests and reformulates the argument (*Just and Unjust Wars*, 152-59).

ing its 1954 Evanston Assembly. A group of fourteen men, all of them from the North Atlantic world, worked for several sessions on the theme "Christians and the Prevention of War in an Atomic Age." Of the fourteen commission members (in addition to Study Department staff), only three could in any way be described as pacifists.

Their report was far ahead of what any Christian bodies in any national or denominational framework were to think for another decade. Their conclusion about the use of nuclear weapons was:

> Although there are differences of opinion on many points, we are agreed on one point. This is that Christians should openly declare that the all-out use of these weapons should never be resorted to. Moreover, that Christians must oppose all policies which give evidence of leading to all-out war. Finally, if all-out war should occur, Christians should urge a cease-fire, if necessary on the enemy's terms, and resort to non-violent resistance.[18]

This wording was logically irreproachable, in fact inevitable, as an application of the ordinary meaning of the just-war tradition, but it was so threatening politically that the study process was terminated. Yet the logic was clear, and it has never been refuted on its own terrain. If it is not possible to prosecute a war with moral and civil legitimacy, then the only alternative is not to prosecute it. The only remaining path is to pursue by other means the purpose which can no longer be legitimately achieved militarily.

Sue for Peace?

This has led us to the crudest form of the credibility question. Is there a point at which it would be morally and legally

---

[18]Quoted here from the 1957 original. The point is less clear in the toned-down version *Christians and the Prevention of War in an Atomic Age*, ed. Robert. S. Bilheimer and Thomas Taylor (London: SCM Press, 1961). This passage is not included in the excerpt from the same report in Donald Durnbaugh, ed., *On Earth Peace* (Elgin, Penn.: Brethren Press, 1978), 185.

obligatory to surrender rather than wrongfully to go on with a war? Does the doctrine imply that? On the level of common sense and the lay meaning of the just-war tradition, it certainly did and must imply the possibility that the wrongness of a particular battle, weapon, or tactic is so clear that it must be rejected, even at the cost of important sacrifice. This possible negation is a part of the dignity of the tradition. The negation applies most dramatically and globally when one recognizes that *if* the only way to defend a just cause is by a fundamentally wrong means, *then* it is mandatory to surrender and to seek to pursue further the defense of one's valid interests through means other than the belligerent defense of natural sovereignty. If this has not been recognized, and plans befitting such an insight have not been made, that is because the just-war heritage has itself not been clearly understood by those claiming to hold to it.

The clearest statement to the effect that the just-war tradition has not been applied by the major political actors in recent Western experience has come not from pacifists but from the most qualified interpreters of that tradition. Paul Ramsey, the preeminent Protestant author in the field, made this very point:

> The test is whether we are willing to limit ends and means in warfare and yet sustain the burden of this evil necessity, whether we as a people are willing, if war comes, to *accept defeat when our fighters cannot win the hoped-for victory rather than venture more and exact more than the nature of just endurable warfare requires,* whether we can mount the resources for action with at most small effect and plan surrender when none is possible [emphasis added].[19]

Another witness is John Courtney Murray, S.J., author of numerous writings in the field, clearly the most qualified Roman Catholic voice of his generation. Murray explained widespread distrust for the doctrine on the grounds of its long disuse:

---

[19]Paul Ramsey, *War and Christian Conscience* (Durham, N.C.: Duke University Press, 1961), 151f.

That is, it has not been made the basis for a sound critique of public policies and as a means for the formation of a right public opinion. The classic example, of course, was the policy of "unconditional surrender" during the last war. This policy clearly violated the requirement of the "right intention" that has always been a principle in the traditional doctrine of war. Yet no sustained criticism was made of the policy by Catholic spokesmen. Nor was a substantial effort made to clarify by moral judgment the thickening mood of savage violence that made possible the atrocities of Hiroshima and Nagasaki. I think it is true that the traditional doctrine was irrelevant during World War II. This is no argument against the traditional doctrine. The Ten Commandments do not lose their imperative relevance by reason of the fact that they are violated. But there is place for an indictment of all of us who failed to make the tradition relevant.[20]

Murray not only let the doctrine speak honestly to condemn what the political authorities of his nation had done, but he also drew the honest and logical conclusion that if the tradition is to be respected, it must set a limit to what a nation is willing to do in order to win. This must mean concretely defining the point at which it is morally imperative to sue for peace.

On grounds of the moral principle of proportion the doctrine supports the grave recommendation of the greatest theorist of war in modern times, von Clausewitz: "We must therefore familiarize ourselves with the thought of an honorable defeat." . . . "Losing," said von Clausewitz, "is a function of winning," thus stating in his own military idiom the moral calculus described by traditional moral doctrine. The moralist agrees with the military theorist that the essence of a military situation is uncertainty. And when he requires, with Pius XII, a solid probability of success as a moral ground for a legitimate use of arms, he must reckon

---

[20] Murray, "Remarks on the Moral Problem of War," 53-54.

with the possibility of failure and be prepared to accept it. But this is a moral decision, worthy of a man and of a civilized nation. It is a free, morally motivated, and responsible act, and therefore it inflicts no stigma of dishonor.[21]

Murray was no defeatist and no pacifist. He insisted that surrender is not the first but the last possibility. The just-war tradition assumes that there can be justifiable ways to wage war, even in modern times. Yet Murray had the integrity to insist that the entire argument is sustainable only if and in so far as those who hold to it do in fact set a limit beyond which they would abandon the military defense of their goals. That may never mean the annihilation of the enemy, nor need it (in the case of a war which may justifiably be waged) demand one's own surrender.

> Surrender may be morally tolerable; but it is not to be tolerated save on a reasonable calculus of proportionate moral costs. In contrast, annihilation is on every count morally intolerable; it is to be averted at all costs.[22]

It is thus undeniable that for some nonpacifists a mandatory cease-fire point is dictated by loyalty to the just-war tradition.[23]

The simplest functional definition of the just-war tradition "with teeth" is that one would rather sue for peace than commit certain legally or morally illicit belligerent acts. If the only way not to lose a war is to commit a war crime, it is morally right to lose that war. If that is intended seriously, there will be moral teaching and technical contingency planning in preparation for that extreme eventuality. If that possibility is not affirmed by someone, that person or community has not yet faced the basic

---

[21] Ibid., 55. I have not been able to locate these particular phrases in Clausewitz, but there is no doubt that Murray has the thought of Clausewitz right. The criterion of "probable success" mentioned by Murray is a traditional one. Murray refers specifically to Pius XII only because he had been reviewing recent papal statements earlier in the article.

[22] Ibid., 56.

[23] See John Howard Yoder, "Surrender: A Moral Imperative," Review of Politics 48 (Fall 1986), 576ff.

moral issue, and we do not yet know that it will not use the notion of necessity arbitrarily.

Category Slide

One of the most frequent ways of undercutting the critical potential of the just-war tradition is to narrow attention to only one or the other of the criteria. Robert Tucker has in fact identified as a specifically American temptation the idea that only the criterion of just cause really matters.[24] This describes both 1914 and 1939. We try to stay out of a war until it is very clear to us that we know whom to blame. Then we want to plunge in and fight without restraint, to win at all costs. To say it technically, considerations of *jus ad bellum* are given such weight that, once satisfied, they threaten to override the restraints of *jus in bello*. If the cause that is at stake is great enough, some of the ordinary restraints may be disregarded in order to win soon and decisively.[25] It may be a weakness of the entire just-war tradition that it permits such selective application.

It is also possible to avoid considering all the criteria by looking in the other direction. Many contemporaries say that since the rise of theologies of revolution it is no longer possible to ask the question of just authority, or that since the rise of the notion of national sovereignty it is no longer possible to ask about just cause (since every nation is judge in its own case). Thus we are reduced to being able to ask only the questions of discrimination—proportion and immunity. We can ask only the most formal questions, since for the others no one has the authority to answer.[26]

In a backhanded way this argument has some value. It keeps people from saying that since their own cause is just, they need

---

[24] Robert W. Tucker, *The Just War: A Study in Contemporary American Doctrine* (Baltimore: Johns Hopkins University Press, 1960), esp. 11ff. President Bush reasoned publicly in this mode concerning the Gulf War.

[25] Another way to characterize this pattern would be that it uses just-war thinking *ad bellum* and then becomes "realist." The language of just war is thereby co-opted but has no restraining power once the threshold is crossed.

[26] Thus Ramsey argued that since we can never agree about legitimate authority or just cause, we can only regulate means.

not be restrained by the rules *in bello*. Restraints *in bello* have to remain in effect against us, assuming our cause is just, as protection for our adversaries' natural rights, even if their cause is unjust. That does not mean, however, that Christian moral responsibility can avoid the questions of moral evaluation on the levels of authority and cause merely by saying that all the parties to the conflict are biased. It is precisely for situations in which people are biased that we need the appeal to common ("natural") criteria. It is precisely because people are biased that we have wars that need to be restrained. The multiple rooting of Christian moral thought—in the thought of the ages, in the goals of rational critical discourse, and in the awareness of world community—should enable asking the hard questions, including the debatable issues of authority and cause, even if the other parties to the conflict are not willing to face them.

Meta-morality

Thus far we have been proceeding on the basis of the ordinary understanding of the just-war tradition as intended to provide moral guidance for decision-makers in government and in combat. The "sliding" we have documented in many forms was articulated in "realistic" terms used to justify exceptions and to explain trade-offs on that level. There is however a more philosophical or academic level on which the binding authority of the rules can be challenged. James Childress[27] argues that what he calls a "substantive" just-war tradition, which could give concrete guidance or impose precise demands, is impossible in a pluralistic world with competing theories of value. In a pluralistic world people will never agree on what is a just government or a just cause. Therefore there can never be a clear *no* to an unjust war in our modern, pluralistic world. Yet Childress holds that the tradition is nevertheless usable. As a formal theory it provides a common language with which to debate.

---

[27]This is James Childress's point about the limited validity of the whole system, and Paul Ramsey's on our inability to judge just cause objectively. James Childress, "Just War Criteria," in Thomas A. Shannon, ed., *War or Peace* (Maryknoll, N.Y.: Orbis Books, 1980), 151ff. Also in James Childress, *Moral Responsibility in Conflicts: Essays on Nonviolence, War, and Conscience* (Baton Rouge: LSU Press, 1982). The essay is reprinted frequently in anthologies.

There have been dozens of variants within just-war thought in the past. No one can deny Childress the freedom to create yet another. Yet in the measure in which he takes that freedom, he forsakes the claim to be interpreting a classical moral tradition. That the classical tradition (moral and legal) includes the possibility of concrete normative negative answers, regarding the admissibility of specific belligerent acts, has always, especially in our pluralistic modern times, been evidenced by:

- The prosecution of war crimes;
- The founding of one nation's claims to just cause and reprisal in the objective wrongness of offenses committed by the other side;
- The possibility of surrender in the just-war thought of John Courtney Murray, Paul Ramsey, and the World Council of Churches commission[28];
- The possibilities of civil disobedience, disobedience to unjust orders, and selective conscientious objection.

In favor of Childress's relativism it is still possible to appeal to other differences, lay or sophisticated, perhaps between the citizen and the politician, or between the idealist and the realist. It can be argued that some restraint is always better than none, even if the rules are never *fully* respected. It may be better for the enemy population if we respect only some of the just-war restraints than if we respected none of them. But what I am asking about here is not about the greater or lesser disutility, for victims, of this or that way of being killed. I am concerned for the moral claims being made for the killers. In some respects the hypocritical claim to be exercising real restraint, when in fact there is none, may do more harm than outright honest "realism."[29] All such arguments in favor of relativism belong to the unavoidable complexity of public moral discourse; I have no

---

[28] See, for example, Ramsey, *War and Christian Conscience*. Childress would not deny that these figures largely merit the credit for restoring the viability of just-war reasoning in this century.

[29] In the 1991 Gulf War the coalition forces' publicity made much of their careful respect for *some* of the just-war restraints. There was no recognition of those rules which were not respected. See below, pages 93f., for the lessons some draw from the Gulf War.

intention to avoid them. My point is that in most cases they diminish rather than heighten the capacity of just-war thought to provide effective moral guidance.

By now the reader will have discerned the drift of our culture. The person who is concerned to give a fair hearing, open-mindedly and critically, to the claim that the just-war tradition is a usable structure of moral accountability was first told that the just-war tradition agrees that war is an evil. Only under the circumstances stated by the criteria evolved over centuries can participation in that evil be justified, on the grounds that (as the application of the criteria serves to verify or falsify) it is less than the evil it prevents. Those criteria are supposed to guarantee that there is no *carte blanche*; there are some things one would never do, even for a just cause.

But then when we ask about the firmness with which the criteria apply, we discover that they keep sliding farther down the scale. With each concession the claim is renewed that this still does not mean that "anything goes." Indeed,

- The double-effect argument is still subject to criteria;
- Reprisals are still subject to proportionality;
- Relaxing some rules is done in order to safeguard the idea of law as such;
- The rules will never be met, but if we keep talking about them the infractions will not be as bad as if we don't;
- We have no common notion of what compliance would mean, or what must never happen, but at least we have a common vocabulary.

The slippery slope pattern is obvious.

Retreats or Routs?

Does the tradition lay a reliable foundation for common discussion and possible common decision about admissible levels of damage that political imperatives may oblige responsible decision-makers to accept without becoming immoral? What seems on closer scrutiny actually to be going on is a series of what we are told are strategic retreats, but they turn out not to be that. A strategic retreat is a sober decision to take some loss, stepping back to a line which may be more firmly defended. That is what *seems* at first to be happening when someone begins the discussion saying that concessions will need to be made (just this once), but only in cases of last resort, self-defense, and so on. That sounds like a line that would be easier to defend than the prohibition of all killing. But when it comes to defending that line, we discover that other reasons are being alleged for stepping back still farther:

- The law will not be respected if we make it too demanding;
- We cannot be expected to stand by all the niceties of the law if the enemy does not;
- Sometimes the best defense may be a preemptive aggression, when the enemy's threat is the moral equivalent of an actual attack.

What had been presented as a line that could be defended now has several degrees of concessions to whatever recourse the most pessimistic picture of the conflict enables someone to claim is necessary. What claimed to be a firm structure for moral discernment has turned spongy. What claimed (in contrast to the intrinsic values served by pacifism or the holy war) to be a toolkit of resources for fine-tuned discrimination turns out in most of the cases we can find in the literature to have been special pleading.

In short, when we give the just-war system a chance to prove its integrity, to prove that a strategic retreat was authentically that by being able more effectively to hold the new lower line, it does not deliver.

Counter to the standard history,[30] the just-war position is not the one which has been taken practically by most Christians since Constantine. Most Christians (baptized people) in most wars since pacifism was forsaken have died and killed in the light of thought patterns derived from the crusade or the national-interest pattern. Some have sought to cover and interpret this activity with the rhetoric of the just-war heritage; others have not bothered. The just-war tradition remains prominent as a consensus of the stated best insights of a spiritual and intellectual elite, who used that

---

[30] For example, *The Challenge of Peace* (Washington, D.C.: U.S. Catholic Conference, 1983).

language as a tool for moral leverage on sovereigns for whom the language of the gospel carried no conviction. Thus just-war rhetoric and consistent pacifism are on the same side of most debates. When honest, both will reject most wars, most causes, and most strategies being prepared and implemented.

How then did the notion that the just-war tradition is the mainstream position remain alive at all? Certainly it is not only that people were misled as to the power of theologians to get a hearing. Certainly there have been both ideal visions and real models of Christian statesmanship and civil heroism. There have been people who, in the exercise of public responsibility, saved or created nations, kept the blood-thirstiness of war from getting out of control, and made some kind of peace through limited power, with restraint, wisdom, and magnanimity. The closer one comes to the domestic model, where restrained violence is like that of the police officer, the more applicable, by analogy, is the just-war language, and the more credible is its claim to be providing real guidance. Those persons who incarnate domestic order and who succeed in imposing social peace from positions of power may have more to do with making believable the idea of subjecting violence to restraint than do actual experiences in war between nations.

The Faith Was Often Different

Not only was the just-war tradition not really in charge in history, but it was not dominant in spirituality. When a history of thought is based on the writings of a magisterial elite, then it is the just-war tradition which we must report. But how many people like that were there, and how many more drew spiritual sustenance from them?

If, on the other hand, we were to ask how through the centuries most people—who were at the same time somehow authentic Christian believers and lived their lives of faith with some explicit sincerity—thought about war, then we should have to report that their lives were sincerely burdened, not nourished, by the just-war grid. Their lives were nourished, not by the summas of the academicians, but by the lives of the saints. Most of the saints were tacitly nonviolent. Most of the martyr-saints were expressly nonviolent. The rejection of violent self-defense or of service in the armies of Caesar was sometimes the reason for which the saint was martyred. The lives of the saints are told to incite the hearer to trust God for his or her surviving and prospering. Even those saints (like Francis) who lived in the midst of war and the few who were soldiers were not Machiavellian. They cultivated a worldview marked by trusting God for survival, a willingness to suffer rather than to sin, and an absence of any cynical utilitarianism in their definition of the path of obedience. The penitent and the pilgrim were normally, naturally defenseless. The stories of the saints abound in tales of miraculous deliverance from the threats of bandits and brigands.

It is a source of deep historical confusion to identify the history of Christian morality as a whole with the record of the thought of academic moralists, where just-war thought in Christendom has been located. Such academic formulations may, in some cultures, make a major contribution to how people will actually make decisions in the future, *if* local preachers or confessors take their cues from the professor. But in other traditions, where the instrument of enforcement that the confessional provides is not used, the relation between the academic articulation and the real life of the community is more like that of the froth to the beer.

CHAPTER 6

Making the Tradition Credible

The preceding review of the ups and downs of history should have made it clear that the just-war tradition is not a simple formula ready to be applied in a self-evident and univocal way. It is rather a set of very broad assumptions whose implications demand—if they are to be respected as morally honest—that they be spelled out in some detail and then tested for their ability to throw serious light on real situations and on the decisions of persons and institutions regarding those situations. We therefore turn to the effort to itemize the resources that would be needed if such authentic implementation were to become a reality.

Intention

Beginning from the inside, we would need to clarify whether in the minds and the hearts of the people using this language there has been a conscious commitment to make the sacrifices required to apply the doctrine negatively. At some time, if the doctrine is not a farce, there would be cases where an intrinsically just cause would have to go undefended militarily because there would be no authority legitimated to defend it. Or an intrinsically just cause defended by a legitimate authority would have to be forsaken because the only way to defend it would be by unjust means. That would be the setting for testing whether citizens or leaders were able in principle to conceive of the sacrifice of that value as morally imperative. Is it something citizens would press on their leaders? Is it reason for the draftee to refuse to serve, or reason for a statesman to negotiate peace?

71

There is no strong evidence for believing that most people using just-war language are ready, either psychically or intellectually, for that serious choice. In popular language—which translates "negotiated peace" as "surrender," proclaims that there is "no substitute for victory," and loosely uses the military language of "necessity" to cover almost any infraction of the laws of war—we have seen the evidence not merely of the high value attributed uncritically to one's own nation or to the righteousness of its cause, but also a profound psychodynamic avoidance mechanism. By refusing to face real options, that avoidance makes it highly unlikely that in undesirable situations there will be any chance of making the hard moral choice.

Last Resort

What constitutes a situation of last resort is not something that can be decided only at the last minute or only by one party. What is decisive to determine whether efforts to resolve political conflicts by means less destructive than war have been adequate will largely depend on whether there was any disposition or plan to attempt to use such prior means in the first place.

During the first decade after Hiroshima the United States could count on its nuclear monopoly to enforce its view of peace around the world; there were not sufficient non-nuclear military means available for effective use in smaller conflicts, so that disproportionate nuclear means threatened to become not the last but the only resort. Similarly, any preoccupation with projecting an image of strength tempts the strong party to leapfrog up the scale past the less destructive recourses.

The United States has been less willing than some other nations to accept in principle the authority of agencies of international arbitration, with the Connally Amendment[1] actually

---

[1] In 1946 the United States Senate passed Resolution 196 concerning the submission of United States international affairs to the jurisdiction of the International Court of Justice. Senator Connally's amendment consisted of six words: "as determined by the United States." That is, we get to determine what is domestic and to be controlled by our courts, and what is not domestic and hence controlled by international justice. In 1984-85 the United States ruled that the mining of harbors in Nicaragua was domestic.

undercutting in a formal way the possibility of recourse to agencies like The Hague International Court of Justice. Even less have we invested in means of conflict resolution on lower levels. We spent forty years sharing with the Soviet Union and China the strategy of escalating local conflicts into surrogates for superpower confrontation, rather than seeking to maximize the authentic independence of non-aligned nations or mediating institutions.

The economic patterns dominating our country have militated against the use of economic and cultural sanctions (positive and negative) to foster international goals, although there have been more efforts (mostly ad hoc, clumsy, and often counterproductive) to use means short of war in some cases.[2] Our international aid agencies hardly have the expertise to administer positive reinforcement in such a way as to diminish recourse to military sanctions without falling prey to new forms of dependency, corruption, and so on. When a government abroad raises any questions about our national interests, we have agencies like the CIA that contribute to escalating rather than diminishing tensions. If we sought to be honest about the restraint on violence implied in the just-war tradition, we would have a nonviolent alternative to the CIA. This would be a creative, non-threatening, information-gathering instrument, which instead of destabilizing regimes it considers unfriendly would find positive means of fostering interdependent development.

Strategies of Nonviolence

Recourse to international agencies of arbitration and mediation as a factor in evaluating when a situation of "last resort" exists is an old idea becoming increasingly pertinent. More attention needs to be given, and has only begun to be given, to a newer development, namely, the rise of aggressive nonviolent strategies for social conflict and change. The impact of Gandhi

---

[2] The cynic observing the reluctance of U.S. legislators and administrators to commit troops in overseas interventions (e.g, Somalia, Bosnia, Haiti) would suggest that it was the product not of just-war scruples but of unwillingness to run risks where strong economic "national interests" would not be served.

and King is only the tip of the iceberg. Besides, beyond, and since them, there have also been:

a) Numerous spontaneous phenomena of non-cooperation with injustice, which have achieved sometimes the desired social change and sometimes a more powerful witness of martyrdom than lashing out with firearms would have done[3];

b) A growing circle of leaders, using similar tactics in their most varied circumstances, most notably and recently:
- the change of government in Manila in February 1986;
- changes of government in Eastern Europe in the fall of 1989 and in Madagascar in 1991; sometimes the recourse to nonviolence was thought through and sometimes it was spontaneous;

c) A growing body of political science literature projecting the serious possibility of attaining without military violence some of the objectives it has previously been claimed could only be attained by war.[4] Nonviolent action on behalf of justice is no automatic formula for success, but neither is war. Most people who go to war for some cause they deem worthy are defeated.[5]

A careful reading of history can find far greater reason than many have previously recognized for expecting nonviolent strategies to be effective. Both anecdotal evidence and social-science analysis have made good beginnings toward projecting and evaluating possible nonmilitary means for defending those values which military means can no longer defend, whether that "no longer" is taken morally or practically.

It is not our task to review that body of literature. If there is available a body of thought and a set of tools of analysis and projection that can respond seriously to the question, How can we defend ourselves if war can no longer do it?, then the situa-

---

[3] Some of these stories are told by Ronald J. Sider, *Nonviolence: The Invincible Weapon?* (Dallas: Word Books, 1989).

[4] See John Howard Yoder, "The Power of Nonviolence," available from the Joan B. Kroc Institute for International Peace Studies, Notre Dame, IN 46556 (document 6:WP:2). (See the bibliography on nonviolent alternatives below.)

[5] Logically speaking, one side in every war is defeated. Often the "victor" is also worse off than before. The classical just-war criterion of probable success is one of the most difficult to honor; it is one of the points where holy or macho reflexes most easily override rational restraint.

tion called last resort cannot be held to obtain. Most of these thinkers are not doctrinaire pacifists.[6] For their arguments to hold water it suffices to agree that war is not justified when it does not achieve its stated aims and when it does more harm than good.

If there are more nonviolent resources available than people have thought about, and if there would be still more available if they *were* thought about, then the conclusion is unavoidable that the notion of last resort—one of the classical criteria of the just-war tradition—must exercise more restraint than it did before.

Authority

The next logical test of the mental readiness of people to live within the limits of honest just-war thinking is at the institutional level. Our government invests millions of staff hours and billions of taxpayers' dollars in developing contingency plans for all possible situations in which the legitimate military prosecution of hostilities would be effective. Where is the contingency planning, where are the thought exercises and training maneuvers for continuing the defense of our values in those situations where military means will not be appropriate? In the 1960s Stephen King-Hall projected the case for defense in a nuclear age needing to be, at least in some cases, nonmilitary.[7] Since then many others have spelled out these possibilities. It cannot be said that the failure of military scientists or political ethicists to respond to King-Hall's challenge is due to the author's not being competent and respected or his argument not being cogent. Whether the avoidance mechanisms that refuse to face this challenge are best analyzed in budgetary, psychodynamic, or political terms, they tend to count against the credibility of those who refuse to respond to the practically formulated challenges of King-

---

[6] See King-Hall, *Defense in a Nuclear Age*. Sir Stephen King-Hall served as instructor in military science in the war colleges of the United Kingdom during World War II. Gene Sharp's numerous publications are based on political realism (see bibliography).

[7] King-Hall, *Defense in a Nuclear Age*.

Hall, Sharp, and the others. Thereby they tend to compromise the credibility of their *pro forma* adherence to the laws of war, and thereby in turn they tend to discredit the coherence of the just-war system itself.

The last few sentences made a backhanded argument. Now I should state the affirmation that corresponds to it. The legitimate authority, which claims the right and the duty to defend the legitimate interests of its citizens (or its allies) by the disciplined and proportionate use of military violence, will be morally credible only when and as it gives evidence of a proportionate investment of creativity and foresight in arrangements to defend those same values by alternate means, in those other contexts in which military means would *not* be morally or legally or technically appropriate. If they are not making those contingency plans, then both their claim that they have the right and duty to use war and their claim that they will do it within the moral limits of the just-war heritage and the legal limits of the laws of war lose credibility.

This awareness that contingency planning for alternative strategies would be a proof of sincerity yields another benefit for our conversation. It tells us that in the measurement of what constitutes last resort, it is not morally sufficient for politicians and strategists to shrug their shoulders and say "we could not think of anything else to do." At least in our times we have the social-science instruments and the intellectual discipline for thinking of alternatives. Last resort can only be claimed when other recourses short of the last have been tested seriously.

Proportion

The reasoning process required by the just-war tradition calls for the evil likely to be caused by warfare to be measured against the evil it hopes to prevent. The critics of the tradition have always wondered what kind of reasoning is going on when one measures various kinds of goods and evils against each other: for example, lives against freedom, or institutions against architecture. We are now trying to wager on the credibility of the tradition. Those who believe that this thought pattern is reliable owe it to their own integrity (and to their potential victims) to possess reliable and verifiable measures of the evil they claim to be warding off and the lesser evil they are willing to commit, albeit reluctantly and without "direct intention."

Such calculation must properly seek to take account not only of specific deeds that one is immediately aware of choosing, but also of the potential for escalation and proliferation which a first step across the threshold of violence can let loose. One would have to factor in the greater or lesser degree of uncertainty with which one can predict both kinds of evils and their causal connection so as to promise just-cause results. Certainly decisions based upon the claimed ability to bring about less evil results, and to do so at the cost of the lives and values of others, need for the sake of one's own integrity to stand up to testing. Such reckoning of proportionality can never be fully certain, but the burden of proof lies with the party who says that it is probable enough to justify intervening by causing some certain lethal evil in order to reduce other projected evils.[8]

Moral Leverage

Thus far I have been describing what institutional instruments would be needed to make the doctrine credible in the sense of applicable. There are however other questions which might come first logically from the perspective of religious moral commitment. Are there people who affirm that their own uncoerced allegiance as believers gives them strength and motivation to honor the restraints of the just-war tradition and to help one another to do so? This might be the only angle from which the development of the needed institutions could be fostered. Would believers commit themselves, and commit themselves to press

---

[8] "If you have the choice between a real evil and a hypothetical evil, always take the hypothetical one" (Joan Baez, "Three Cheers for Grandma!" *Daybreak* [New York: Dial, 1968] and *Atlantic Monthly* [August 1968], cited in J. Yoder, ed., *What Would You Do?* [Scottdale, Penn.: Herald Press, 1992], 63).

each other, to be willing to enter the political opposition, or to resign public office, or to espouse selective objection? Does any church teach future soldiers and citizens in such a way that they will know beyond what point they cannot support an unjust war or use an unjust weapon?

Since the capacity to reach an independent judgment concerning the legality and morality of what is being done by one's rulers depends on information, which by the nature of the case must be contested, does the religious community provide alternative resources for gathering and evaluating information concerning the political causes for which their governments demand their violent support? What are the preparations being made to obtain and verify an adequately independent and reliable source of facts and of analytical expertise, enabling honest dissent to be so solidly founded as to be morally convincing? Is every independent thinker on his or her own, or will the churches support agencies to foster dissent when called for?

Neither the pacifist nor the crusader needs to study in depth the facts of politics in order to make a coherent decision. The person claiming to respect just-war rationality must do so, however, and therefore must have a reliable independent source of information. I have stated this as a question about the church, but it also applies to the society. Is there free debate? Are the information media free? Is opposition legitimate? Does the right of conscientious objection have legal recognition?

Are soldiers when assigned a mission given sufficient information to determine whether this is an order they should obey? If a person under orders is convinced he or she must disobey, will the command structure, the society, and the church honor that dissent? It is reported that in the case of the obliteration bombing of Dresden the pilots were not informed that it could hardly be considered a military target. For most of the rest of the just-war criteria factual knowledge is similarly indispensable.

Until today church agencies on any level have invested little effort in literature or other educational means to teach the just-war limitations. The few such efforts one sees are in no way comparable to the way in which the churches teach their young people about other matters concerning which they believe morality is important, such as sexuality. The understanding of the just-war logic that led American young men to refuse to serve in Vietnam came to them not primarily from the ecclesiastical or academic interpreters of the tradition but rather from the notions of fair play presupposed in our popular culture.[9]

A Fair Test

Those who conclude, either deliberately or rapidly, that in a given situation of injustice there are no nonviolent options available, often do so in a way that avoids responsibility for any intensive search for such options. The military option for which they so quickly reach has involved a long lead time in training and equipping the forces. It demands the preparation of a special class of leadership, for which most societies have special schools and learning experiences. It demands costly special resources dependent on abundant government funding, and it demands broad alliances. It includes the willingness to lose lives and to take lives, to sacrifice other cultural values for a generation or more, and the willingness of families to be divided.

Yet the decision that nonviolent means will not work for comparable ends is made without any comparable investment of time or creativity, without comparable readiness to sacrifice, and without serious projection of comparable costs. The American military forces would not "work" if we did not invest billions of dollars in equipping, planning, and training. Why should it be fair to measure the moral claims of an alternative strategy by setting up the debate in such a way that that other strategy should have to promise equivalent results with far less financial investment and less planning on every level? The epigram of the 1960s—People give nonviolence two weeks to solve their prob-

---

[9] Like the morality plays of medieval Europe, the police thriller and the western in our culture are the primary instruments of moral education. That the good guy does not shoot first, that innocents should not be killed, and that the good guy wins in the end even though (or even because) he fights by the rules, are staples of that narrative moral instruction.

lems and then say it has failed; they've gone on with violence for centuries, and it seems never to have failed—is not a pacifist argument. It is a sober self-corrective within just-war reasoning.

In sum, the challenge should be clear. If the tradition which claims that war may be justified does not also admit that in particular cases it may *not* be justified, the affirmation is not morally serious. A Christian who prepares the case for a justifiable war without being equally prepared for the negative case has not soberly weighed the *prima facie* presumption that any violence is wrong until the case for the exception has been made. We honor the moral seriousness of the nonpacifist Christian when we spell out the criteria by which the credibility of that commitment, shaped in the form of the just-war system, must be judged.

CHAPTER 7

The Changing Face of the Problem

The last generation has seen great growth in the attention given to just-war thought patterns, both in society at large and in Christian circles. Opinions will vary as to whether this increases the effectiveness of the just-war tradition as an instrument or effective restraint. In any case the developments are weighty, and they illustrate the relevance of our theme.

This chapter shall attend first to developments in specifically Roman Catholic thought, which have proceeded gradually toward enhancing the critical potential of the tradition.

John Courtney Murray, S.J., and World War II Revisited

Although numerous thinkers, church leaders, and journalists were immediately critical of the nuclear bombing of Japan, it took a decade for it to become the topic of full critical attention by theologians. This critique is best represented for our purpose by John Courtney Murray, S.J., the nation's most respected Roman Catholic moral theologian. Murray's intention was not to critique the just-war tradition but to retrieve it, saving it from two dominant misunderstandings; namely, that the just-war system had been rendered irrelevant by modern war, and that it was responsible for justifying what modern war had become. Murray was sure that such a retrieval was both possible and imperative. Looking back at World War II, his belief led him to disagree firmly with the national consensus, especially, as we saw earlier, at the following points:

81

a) He rejected the stated war goal of demanding unconditional surrender from the enemy.[1]

b) He condemned the refusal to consider surrender as a possibility for the United States in case a war could not be won without fighting unjustly.[2]

c) He condemned the nuclear bombing of Hiroshima and Nagasaki.[3] Murray did not enter into comparison or contrast with the other massive city bombings of World War II, but one must assume that his reasons would have been those already stated by John Kenneth Ryan in 1934 and by John Ford, S.J., in 1944,[4] and that he would have said the same things about the earlier attacks on Hamburg, Dresden, Tokyo, and the smaller German and Japanese cities which were treated no differently.

Although Murray argued with great clarity and cogency for the classical criteria, his report honestly went on to add that secular political thinkers were moving away from rather than toward that classical base line, seeking not to narrow but to

---

[1] As we saw in chapter 5, this was always part of the traditional criterion of right intention. Unconditional surrender had become an Allied objective in World War II in an odd way. President Franklin Roosevelt announced it as a war goal in a press conference after the Casablanca summit (January 1943), although it had not been part of his negotiations with Churchill and Stalin. It complicated significantly the negotiations for Japan's surrender. Murray's point is not that it was politically costly, however, but that it was morally wrong.

[2] As we saw in chapter 5, this was part of the classical criterion of probable success, but it was often neglected. This conviction led Murray to condemn a law which had just been passed by the U.S. Congress (which is still on the books) forbidding U.S. military strategists to do any contingency planning concerning suing for peace (see Yoder, "Surrender: A Moral Imperative").

[3] John Courtney Murray, "Remarks on the Moral Problem of War," *Theological Studies* 20 (1959), 40-61. Murray's text also circulated in pamphlet form and in anthologies (sometimes under the title "Theology and Modern War"). Very similar arguments were presented almost simultaneously by the leading Protestant authority in the same field, Paul Ramsey of Princeton, by a study committee of the World Council of Churches, the international ecumenical agency created in 1949, and by a German Protestant movement called *Kirchliche Bruderschaften*.

[4] Ford, "The Morality of Obliteration Bombing," 261-309; and Ryan, *Modern War and Basic Ethics*.

widen the room for exceptionally acceptable use of nuclear arms.

Vietnam and the Issue of Citizen Responsibility

The nation's experience with the war in Korea seems to have provoked little new thought about the moral principles at stake. Vietnam, however, was different in many ways, and it was natural that just-war concepts were called upon to articulate the rising doubts of citizens and church leaders. For instance,

- Could one claim legitimate authority in the United States without a congressional declaration of war? Did President Eisenhower act as a legitimate authority when he decided unilaterally to break the commitment of the Geneva Accords, which would have let the people of Vietnam decide their fate by free elections?
- Could one claim legitimate authority in South Vietnam, when its government was a corrupt dictatorship no more popular than the one in the North?
- Could one claim the ultimate intention of peace when the real adversary was thought to be world communism?
- Could the war ever be won and thus meet the criterion of probability of success?
- Was the war being fought with legitimate means?
- Are burning napalm and phosphorus inhumane weapons?
- Is it possible in that kind of war to respect noncombatant immunity?

Our concern here is not to evaluate U.S. policies in Vietnam but to take note of what language was used to discuss them. The Vietnam experience provoked a weighty renewal of sensitivity to the issues the just-war criteria evaluate. It was also the first time that large numbers of Americans, while not pacifists, made their own decisions about the legitimacy of the war and refused to serve in it, basing their decisions on just-war considerations.[5]

---

[5] See Yoder, "The Moral Responsibility to Refuse to Serve in an Unjust War."

Pope John XXIII and the Cuban Missile Crisis

In October 1962, after the Bay of Pigs invasion attempt, U.S. information services verified that the Soviet Union was supplying Cuba with missiles that could reach much of the United States. The Kennedy administration threatened nuclear attack against the Soviet Union if the missiles were not withdrawn. The immediate U.S. objective was achieved, although at the cost of the increased polarization of the world between the superpowers.[6]

In response to this threat Pope John XXIII, moving more rapidly and more on his own than is often the case in the preparation of such documents, released on Holy Thursday, April 11, 1963, his last major encyclical, *Peace on Earth*.[7]

Peace on Earth was widely recognized as a new level of communication with the world of nations beyond the Roman Catholic Church.[8] Very little of this letter is directly about war. None of it is about the details of applying just-war principles. Yet the categorical statement that "it is contrary to reason to hold that war is now a suitable way to restore rights which have been violated" anchored the seriousness of the letter's description of the proper rights and relationships of persons in civil community and the relationships between peoples. It thereby set the stage for the treatment of the war question by the Second Vatican Council, which John XXIII had already set in motion.

---

[6] Because Kennedy made his decisions without consulting the NATO allies, France withdrew from NATO. And because Khrushchev backed down, he was replaced as Soviet premier by someone tougher.

[7] David J. O'Brien and Thomas A. Shannon, eds., *Catholic Social Thought: The Documentary Heritage* (Maryknoll, N.Y.: Orbis Books, 1992).

[8] An excellent description of how this text differed from other papal documents, and how widely it was received, is provided by David J. O'Brien and Thomas A. Shannon in *Renewing the Earth: Catholic Documents on Peace, Justice, and Liberation* (Garden City: Doubleday Image, 1977), 117ff.

Vatican Council II

Gaudium et Spes (*The Church in the Modern World*), December 7, 1965,[9] was the product of the work of Vatican II on the broad scope of Christian concern for social values. All of culture is addressed: marriage and the family, the economy, education, and many other topics. Here we are concerned only with "The Fostering of Peace and the Promotion of a Community of Nations" (chapter 5). There are numerous passing references to war that go beyond earlier statements,[10] yet there is no unrealistic idealism:

> As long as . . . there is no competent and sufficiently powerful authority at the international level, governments cannot be denied the right to legitimate defense. . . . [Yet it is] something else again to seek the subjugation of other nations. Nor does the possession of war potential make every . . . use of it lawful. Neither does the mere fact that war has unhappily begun mean that all is fair between the warring parties (par. 81).[11]

Under the heading "Total War" the strongest and most-quoted restraining statement is made:

> Any act of war aimed indiscriminately at the destruction of entire cities or of extensive areas along with their population is a crime against God and man himself. It

---

[9] In O'Brien and Shannon, *Renewing the Earth*, 171ff.

[10] For example: (a) These teachings are founded not only on general affirmations of human community but also on the imperative of loving the enemy (par. 28); (b) they call for the refusal of obedience to unjust orders (par. 79); and (c) the affirmation of provisions for conscientious objectors (par. 79).

[11] This section has been quoted in the recently-released *Catechism of the Catholic Church* (par. 2308).

merits unequivocal and unhesitating condemnation (par. 80).[12]

Broad critical attention is addressed to the dangers of the arms race, the imperative of disarmament, the development of agencies of international cooperation, international development aid, and the duty of Christian involvement in all of these concerns. The text calls for "a completely fresh reappraisal of war" (ibid.), without indicating precisely in what the requisite freshness should consist.

In October 1965, after the Council's work was done but before *Gaudium et Spes* was promulgated, Pope Paul VI spoke in his own name to the Assembly of the United Nations in New York:

> Not the ones against the others, never again, never more. . . . The blood of millions . . . useless slaughter and frightful ruin are the sanction of the pact which unites you, with an oath which must change the future history of the world: No more war, war never again!
>
> Peace, it is peace which must guide the destinies of people and of all mankind.

The Challenge of Peace

Various sources contributed through the late 1970s to the rise of concern about the escalation of the nuclear arms race. The National Council of Catholic Bishops called in 1980 for a study process, led by a committee of five bishops, with unprecedentedly wide consultation and research,[13] resulting finally in the issu-

---

[12] The statement is introduced dramatically by alluding to "the condemnations of total war already pronounced by recent popes," and by the transition, "issues the following declaration."

[13] See Jim Castelli, *The Bishops and the Bomb* (Garden City: Doubleday Image, 1983); George Weigel, *Tranquilitas Ordinis* (New York: Oxford University Press, 1987), 257-85.

ance of the pastoral letter *The Challenge of Peace: God's Promise and Our Response.*[14]

The Challenge of Peace demands interpretation as a historic event in several ways. Its significance is not limited to what it says about the just-war tradition.

The Challenge of Peace *as Ecclesiastical Event*

Formally, this study was a largely unprecedented phenomenon in the life of the Roman Catholic Church in America, as institution. Only after Vatican II was it possible for a regional or national body of bishops to deliberate together on matters of fundamental principle. Nationwide Catholic agencies had been active for years and had been represented at Washington in education, in some lobbying in the interest of Catholic values, but seldom in studying new and difficult themes, and seldom in this length and depth.[15]

It was a new idea that, as a result of study on regional and national levels, there might be points at which bishops in different parts of the world would come to different conclusions. This did in fact happen with regard to some dimensions of the theme. In the German Federal Republic and in France, at about the same time, other episcopal documents were being written which were less critical of the deterrent use of the nuclear threat.[16] A further innovation was distinguishing between levels of the bishops' teaching authority, inviting critical response on those levels of the argument based upon readings of the concrete situation (par. 5-12).

---

[14] Washington, D.C.: National Conference of Catholic Bishops, 1983. See also, O'Brien and Shannon, *Catholic Social Thought.* As this text has been reproduced in many formats, citations are by paragraph rather than by page number.

[15] A partial precedent had been the nationwide network of hearings whereby the bishops took note of the nation's bicentennial, resulting in a 1976 conference at Detroit and a "call to action" concerning matters of social concern.

[16] The bishops of France and West Germany said "to threaten is not to use." For *The Challenge of Peace*, the threat includes the intention to use (under certain circumstances which are under the control of others) and is therefore unacceptable.

It was significant, though not utterly without precedent, that the study process arose in response to the concern of laity; persons working in arms factories or demonstrating against the nuclear-armed submarines were given a respectful hearing by the bishops.

As has seldom happened in the past in such a formal way, *The Challenge of Peace* used the negative potential ("teeth") of the just-war tradition. It spoke of particular strategies and tactics which under no circumstances could be justified, even though they were currently accepted according to national policy and explicitly rejected nuclear war.

From this it followed that *The Challenge of Peace* signaled a new level of readiness on the part of the bishops, and in some sense of the American Roman Catholic communion as a whole, to speak critically of national policies, even at the cost of appearing unpatriotic.[17]

The letter is very clear that theological and technical concerns interact in complex ways. The committee researched the technical and legal sides of the arms race in depth. Concerning the conclusions to which they came, the bishops explicitly explain that on the different topics they speak with different levels of authority. Readers are free to differ on the kinds of questions where the bishops do not claim a single theological answer.

But our more direct interest in the present study is to see *The Challenge of Peace* as a phenomenon in the history of moral thinking about war. Here too there was significant originality.

The Challenge of Peace *as Moral Guidance*

The Challenge of Peace affirms that pacifism and just war are complementary in their logic; both consider war an evil, although they differ in how that presumption works itself out practically. The two positions also make common cause in political applica-

---

[17]In previous decades American Catholics had very seldom been critical in public of any actions of the federal government, especially in foreign affairs. Vietnam and the changing national climate about abortion have now begun to change this.

tion, in the case where a nation is waging or planning an unjust war (par. 74, 111-21). The beginning biblical and historical review points out that pacifism is in line with the Christian scriptures and the early church, and today the possibilities of nonviolent struggle and of peaceful conflict resolution strengthen the commonalities of the two positions (par. 11ff., 221ff.).[18] The Christian who is a pacifist is not heretical,[19] although pacifist commitments cannot be pressed on others or on a nation. Governments should recognize both pacifist conscientious objection to all war and selective or just-war objection to a particular war (par. 233).[20]

In their account of the history of the issue the bishops do not study the past in depth. They do not name the real errors of the churches in the past, which had in fact proclaimed crusades, blessed "realistic" and "Rambo" wars, and generally failed to apply the just-war restraints.[21]

How The Challenge of Peace *States the Traditional Just-War Criteria*

The usual criteria *ad bellum* are listed (par. 85-99) without discussing whether U.S. policies measured up to them.[22]

---

[18]The complementarity theme has been challenged especially in Weigel, *Tranquilitas Ordinis*, and in Kenneth Himes, "Pacifism and the Just War Tradition in Roman Catholic Social Teaching," in *One Hundred Years of Catholic Social Thought*, ed. John A. Coleman, S.J. (Maryknoll, N.Y.: Orbis Books, 1991), 329-44. Norbert Rigali is critical as well ("Just War and Pacifism," *America* 150/123 [1984]: 233-36).

[19]As we saw above, however, the mainstream Protestant reformers did raise pacifism to the status of heresy; it is wrong according to their respective confessions for a Lutheran or an Anglican to be pacifist.

[20]*The Challenge of Peace* argues that the position of the selective objector should be recognized. See Yoder, "The Moral Responsibility to Refuse to Serve in an Unjust War."

[21]John Courtney Murray, S.J. argued bluntly that in recent centuries the just-war doctrine had not been seriously applied ("Remarks on the Moral Problem of War"). *The Challenge of Peace* seems rather to assume without argument that it had always been known, taught, and respected.

[22]Paragraph 100 recognized retrospectively that the Vietnam War was not justified in terms of proportionality. For some reason the two criteria of innocent immunity, which mattered to most of the critics of the war at the time (and which apply most simply to the nuclear threat), and of probable success, which finally convinced the U.S. government to withdraw from Vietnam, are not mentioned.

The insight that last resort includes maximum use of whatever resources of international organization might resolve a conflict is an important Roman Catholic teaching (see also par. 235-44), which the bishops note but to which they give less attention than the popes have done.[23]

"Comparative Justice" (par. 92-94) is listed as a separate criterion. If pursued thoroughly, this consideration might strengthen the restraints *in bello* by recognizing evils on both sides. In this setting, however, the text seems to imply that since "nobody's perfect" our cause need not be irreproachable, as long as the enemy's cause is worse than ours (the communist evil empire[24]). Thereby the effect would be a sliding scale, which would *lower* the standards *ad bellum*. If this was what is meant, (as Michael Novak argued that it should be[25]) and as others have read the passage, it would not be true to the tradition. The intention of author Bryan Hehir, however, was rather to restate the concept—present in the older tradition under other words—that since each side thinks its cause is just, each is obligated to grant the other side's possible good faith and to respect all the other rules, *even though* the adversary is very evil.[26]

Under the criteria *in bello* only two are mentioned by *The Challenge of Peace*, namely, proportion and innocent immunity. They are not enumerated with labeled paragraphs, as were the criteria *ad bellum*, and the three-strand interlock of discrimination/proportion/immunity[27] is not made clear. Discrimination as such is not named, although it is a formal prerequisite for honoring noncombatant immunity and had been the primary concept named in paragraph 80 of *Gaudium et Spes*.

---

[23] See Joseph J. Fahey, "The Catholic Church and the Arms Race," *Worldview* (November 1979), 38-41.

[24] A section on the evils of world communism (par. 248-57) was added to the letter in the third draft.

[25] Michael Novak, *Moral Clarity in the Nuclear Age* (Nashville: Thomas Nelson, 1983). Novak does not *say* that when the enemy is worse you need to be less restrained, but there is no other way to read the implication of his concern to describe especially the evils of the Soviet system.

[26] The reader will note that the impact of this perspective is opposite to that of the "sliding scale."

[27] See the full listing on pages 156-58 below (items VII, VIII, and IX) for the way the three criteria interlock.

Some others of the traditional criteria are missing:

- The criterion of respect for the customs and laws of war. This would draw attention to a large body of treaty law, which includes provisions concerning nuclear arms. It might, if taken seriously, also draw more attention to the fact that the United States is less respectful of international law and international agencies than most modern democracies, and less than Catholic social teachings call for.
- The several criteria traditionally referred to as dictated by "respect for the human dignity of the adversary as a rational being," which in classical Catholic thought forbids lying, perfidy, perjury, mockery, torture, rape, mutilation.
- The criteria related to the common good, present traditionally in specific prohibitions such as those against pillage, mutilating corpses, cutting fruit trees, and poisoning wells. Many, by extension, would apply to nuclear arms.
- Although the Vietnam case is referred to under proportionality, no attention is given to the vast and increasing set of challenges posed in many other zones by so-called low-intensity conflict or other new tactics.
- In addition, *The Challenge of Peace* does not acknowledge the internal problems of how to use a system with multiple criteria. The difficulties of defining some of the criteria are noted but are not clarified.

The Challenge of Peace *and Recent Vatican Teaching*

In addition to these specific cross-references to the rest of just-war thought, we note some differences between the letter and Catholic social thought in general:

- The notion of distinguishing between specifically Christian morality and what makes sense to the wider society, in such a way that only the latter is publicly binding (par. 16), is a modernization. It is especially compatible with just-war thinking, but many Roman Catholic moral thinkers in the past would not have given it this importance.
- Older Catholic moral thought was nourished by the lives of the saints, by the reading of scripture in the liturgy, by works of mercy, and by the cultivation of virtues including meekness

and patience. These tendencies were compatible with renouncing or restraining violence. Dorothy Day, pacifist founder of the Catholic Worker, was no less "Catholic" than her archbishop, Cardinal Spellman.

• There has also been in the past a lot of Catholic nationalism, Catholic ethnocentrism, and Catholic imperialism. The letter gives no attention to how the challenge of war was handled poorly in the past.

The most delicate challenge and the primary focus of concern in the early 1980s are the careful border-walking on nuclear deterrence.[28] Only a real threat, one which will actually be carried out, can deter. Yet only a threat that will *not* be carried out can be reconciled with the criterion of "right intention."[29]

The fine line the 1983 text drew said that while in principle the U.S. deterrent policy currently in effect was unacceptable, because it did presuppose the real intent to harm noncombatants, the short-range retention of that deterrent capability could be condoned, under the strict conditions that the retention was part of a negotiating stance that would lead to its being phased out.

This formulation of the reason for "strictly conditional acceptance" led to a call for review after five years. Was the retention of nuclear weapons in 1983-88 in fact "part of a negotiating stance leading to disarmament"?[30] The fifth-anniversary update tended to refute the "strictly conditioned" claim by keeping the same words on the deterrence question, while the committee

---

[28] The fact that in the mid-1990s this is no longer the most worrisome priority for many does not keep the issue from serving us well here as a specimen for the issues at stake.

[29] See John Howard Yoder, "Bluff or Revenge: The Watershed in Democratic Deterrence Awareness," in *Ethics in the Nuclear Age*, ed. Todd Whitmore (Dallas: AMU Press, 1989), 79-92. Not only innocent immunity is at stake; a second strike also sins against other just-war criteria. This is the point where the French and German bishops differed, they claimed that the credible threat could be morally separated from the intention to carry it out.

[30] Cardinal Krol, testifying to a congressional committee, said, in effect, "If you don't make progress in disarming, we may have to withdraw the condoning of the present state of affairs" (paraphrased). But governments did not make progress and the bishops did not withdraw the condoning. Reported in *Origins* 9 (September 13, 1979), 195-99.

found no way to say that the United States was in fact working to dismantle the threat.

The bishops' subsequent document, *The Harvest of Justice Is Sown in Peace*,[31] issued ten years later, moved on with the same general peacemaking concern as *The Challenge of Peace*. It did not analyze the just-war criteria in further detail, but strengthened the accent on the spiritual and cultural grounds for a peacemaking commitment by Christians and their magisterium.[32]

The Pope and the Gulf War

One effect of *The Challenge of Peace* was to educate people more widely about the existence of the just-war tradition. The language was much more familiar in the public mind as the country invaded Grenada, then Panama, and finally during the Gulf War of 1990-91.

The efforts of large numbers of concerned people to apply the just-war patterns to the Gulf War made it apparent that the system is not a clear set of self-applying rules. Much of this discussion was not specifically Catholic in setting or character. To that we shall soon proceed. Yet one of the strongest critical responses was from Rome.

"Modern War and Christian Conscience," an unsigned editorial in the Jesuit periodical *La Civilta cattolica* on July 6, 1991, responded to the fruitlessness of Vatican efforts to ward off or mitigate the war.[33] Such editorials, while possessing no official magisterial status, seldom contradict the convictions of the pope. Remembering the call of Vatican II for "a completely fresh appraisal of war with an entirely new mentality" (*Gaudium et Spes*, par. 80), the editorial reviewed the varied attitudes of Catholics toward war over the centuries. While accepted by most theolo-

---

[31] National Council of Catholic Bishops (NCCB), *The Harvest of Justice Is Sown in Peace* (Washington, D.C.: USCC, 1994). Also available in *Origins* 23/26 (December 9, 1993), 450-64.

[32] See the review of the themes of *The Harvest of Justice Is Sown in Peace* by D. Christiansen, pages 102-17 below.

[33] Translated in *Origins* 21 (December 1991), 450-55.

gians in recent centuries, the just-war theory, it said, was never made binding by the magisterium. The intent of the theory was not to justify war but to restrain it, yet in modern war the conditions it sets are unattainable. Now that war has become "total," no war can be conducted according to the criteria required. Both the concept of natural sovereignty and the technology of modern warfare are by their nature not subject to restraint. The Gulf War had a just motive, namely, counteracting an aggression, but "by its own inexorable inner logic" it escalated and inflicted unjustifiable levels of damage. Thus the theory is "untenable and needs to be abandoned." The only justified war would be "pure defense against an aggression actually taking place." There are other remedies for the injustices war seeks to rectify.

This Roman text can be taken as representative of many voices speaking of revision in that:

a) It confirms that when the just-war thought pattern took over Christian moral theology in the West centuries ago, it was a powerful intellectual consensus but not a normative definition of dogma by the magisterium. Such a definition, fitting the rules for binding magisterial definition, has never been made.

b) When someone states that the just-war theory is unacceptable, the argument is often one which accepts the criteria as valid and then says that in our world they cannot be met. This means that one is actually using the theory, in a context where the judgment it produces on a particular war must be negative. Thus just-war thinking is not replaced by another view (e.g., by pacifism or "realism").

c) There is no intention to retract the readiness for war in the ideal prototype case of self-defense.

d) The ideal appeal to institutions of world order, which, if they existed, ought to make war unnecessary, avoids coming to grips with the tragic choice of martyrdom when the good is authentically overwhelmed.

Non-Catholic Parallels on the Level of Ordinary Discourse

Alan Geyer and Barbara Green, using the standard just-war concepts as part of their argument, also emphasized the inadequacy of the system.[34] Their summary was based on wide acquaintance with the public discussion in secular and religious journalism at the time of the Gulf War. They point out that just-war thinking

- tends to obscure the ambiguity of justice claims in conflicts where typically both sides are responsible. This oversimplification was clearly present in the Gulf War, in the notion that the invasion of Kuwait by Iraq had settled clearly the cause question.
- tends to avoid the imperative of repentance, which is a precondition for reconciliation and self-restraint; thereby it fosters self-righteousness.
- tends to respond only to one episode instead of seeing events in historic continuity.[35]
- tends to assume that justice and love are alternatives, with love being less relevant, thus relegating moral obligations to some other world.
- condemns overt military action but not other (systemic, institutional) evils.
- credits the *intention* to avoid targeting the innocent without holding belligerents responsible for actual disproportionate and/or indiscriminate *consequences*, undervaluing the suffering caused by calling it collateral or unintended.
- tends to rationalize the claims of the powerful that their might makes right.
- tends to facilitate unilateral action in an age when decisions should be shared.

We may note that while each of these observations implies a serious limitation to the adequacy of just-war thinking, they do not sweep it aside in favor of pacifism, realism, or something else. If carefully taken account of, these considerations would contribute to a much more refined and dense just-war analysis, which could issue in a heightened capacity for restraint and a

---

[34] Alan Geyer and Barbara Green, *Lines in the Sand: Justice and the Gulf War* (Louisville: Westminster/John Knox Press, 1993).

[35] Geyer and Green compare this to an umpire who penalizes one punch, which he saw thrown, but not the one which provoked it.

greater capacity to refuse to give one's own government a blank check.

Walter Wink, another well-documented and empathetic interpreter, names the following shortcomings:

- No Christian body has ever used the just-war criteria to declare unjust any war in which its government was engaged.
- No war Christians have supported has in fact met the just-war requirements.
- No deliberative process appealing to the repertory of just-war criteria has taken place in the lead-up to any of the major wars of the West.
- The decisive criteria have no clear and objective definition; for example,
  —What is "legitimate authority" in settings of guerrilla insurgency?
  —If "aggression" is always wrong, who really started this particular conflict?
  —Does democracy change the definition of who the combatants are?
  —Does "total war" change the definition of noncombatancy?

The logic for the use of the criteria is loose:

- Do they all have to be met?
- Do some outweigh others? If so, how to calculate that?
- Can anything be done about both parties reading the criteria in their own favor?[36]

Academic Analysis

As representative of academic thought on the same subject, we may select one of the more full and prestigious recent arguments in the *Harvard International Law Review*. Christ af Jochnick and Roger Norman argue that when national governments negotiated the treaties providing for the regulation of war, the provision for exceptions justified by "necessity" makes the

---

[36]Walter Wink, *Engaging the Powers* (Minneapolis: Fortress Press, 1991), 212ff. Despite these criticisms, Wink is willing to keep appealing to the criteria, not to justify a war but to minimize violence.

entire process deceptive; it justifies war more than it restrains it.[37]

Another essay by these authors in the same journal refers to the disregard for civilian life and health, and the long-range destruction inflicted on the economic infrastructure of Iraq during the 1991 Gulf War in order to demonstrate that the theoretical principles the laws of war are supposed to implement are illusory. The rules do not actually impose effective restraint.[38]

As we noted concerning Geyer and Green, so too in these papers the authors demonstrate the weaknesses of the dominant usage of international law as an implementation of the just-war tradition, but they do not replace it with pacifism or realism. Rather, by the very way they point to inadequacies, they call for a more detailed and especially a more objective use of the same critical principles, which if more adequately implemented would restrain war more effectively, yet without flipping over into pacifism.

Room for Growth within the System

Here we move beyond the history of our society at large to take note of some possible growing edges in the applicability of just-war thinking.

If the basic attitude underlying the just-war tradition is authentically alive, whereby informed and realistic people take responsibility for restraining public destructiveness by pointing out the worst offenses and filling the gaps in the system, we should naturally expect that the process of development of the just-war conceptual system would never be concluded as long as the present world political arrangement has not changed. We should expect growth both in refining the sensitivity of the concepts at work and in responding to new developments in the nature of war. By way of illustrations currently visible in the 1990s, we

---

[37] Jochnick and Norman, "The Legitimation of Violence: A Critical History of the Laws of War."

[38] Jochnick and Norman, "The Legitimation of Violence: A Critical Analysis of the Gulf War."

may point to two examples of such open edges where more development would be called for.[39] There could well be more examples, all across the agenda.

1) The rejection of public triumphalism. Back at the beginnings of the just-war tradition Augustine commented that the acceptance of any killing was "mournful." Such regret in the face of killing even when justified was implemented by the rituals of penance for killing even in a just war.[40] Discerning observers of the American response to the 1991 Gulf War pointed out that a ticker-tape victory parade celebrated just days after tens of thousands of Iraqi deaths demonstrates that the resort to violence in that case was not reluctant and mournful, as the Christian case for just-war requires, but rather triumphal.[41] The same issue surfaced in Great Britain when some clergy refused to be as happy about the country's victory over Argentina in the war for the Malvinas/Falklands as was Prime Minister Thatcher.

2) Awareness of the way in which land mines keep killing the innocent for years is continuing to grow in recent years. Broadcasting small bombs over fields and forests will have *primarily* the effect of killing and maiming the innocent on into the distant future. That has always been wrong, but the cheapness, the small size, and the long life of modern weapons make the effects far greater. It would be possible to manufacture bombs which deac-

---

[39]Like the above reporting on recent developments, what is weighty about these developments is not the personal insights or convictions of the author, but the fact that the thinking being reported is going on among qualified people concerned to be consistent.

[40]See Bernard J. Verkamp, *The Moral Treatment of Returning Soldiers in Early Medieval and Modern Times* (London/Toronto: Associated University Presses, 1993). Soldiers returning from Vietnam were ostracized once the nation had acknowledged that the war was not righteous. The need was not to say that the war had been just after all, but that sin can be forgiven. Modern understandings of human dignity are not good at that.

[41]Michael J. Schuck, "When the Shooting Stops: Missing Elements in Just War Theory," *Christian Century* (October 26, 1994), 982ff. This astute observation resembles another criterion which, as we noted above, has always been present on the edge of the classical tradition; namely, that the winner should show mercy after victory. This cannot be measured as an operational criterion *ad bellum* or *in bello*, but it can be spoken of as a component of right intention, and it can be revealing after the fact.

tivate themselves after some length of time, but that would be more expensive. There are millions of little bombs still killing and maiming farmers and foresters long after the wars in which they were sown.[42] Enormously costly work is needed to disarm the fields, if it can be done at all.

One form that this awareness takes in international law circles is the effort, being promoted with increasing vigor, to draft new international conventions to outlaw such weapons or their manufacture, obliging their replacement to be short-lived substitutes (bombs which could be just as lethal but which would disarm themselves after a few weeks). More immediate evidence of moral and legal integrity would be that field operations officers would know, without needing a new UN text to educate them, that these are not legitimate weapons for use in settings where most of the victims will be noncombatant. It is a bitter paradox that in the nuclear age one of the highest death tolls, one which rages on for decades after the war is over, is due to the most decentralized and low-tech "bomblet," a minimal weapon that strikes one laborer or child at a time.[43]

Low-Intensity Conflict

Under the specter of nuclear escalation, the strategic thinking of the major powers turned to ways of continuing the world conflict on a smaller scale, using client states to combat as surrogates. The code term *low-intensity conflict* defined this new phase

---

[42] Hunters and foresters in France are still being killed every year by explosives planted in World War I. It was reported by public radio in June 1995 that two million mines have been planted in Croatia in the three years of civil war there. UN information in July 1995 indicated that 110 million live mines are lying around in sixty-four countries, killing thirty thousand persons annually. The USSR planted thirty-five million in Afghanistan alone; ten million are manufactured annually.

[43] A speech given by Pope John Paul II on the fiftieth anniversary of the founding of Pax Christi calls for cessation in the production and deployment of "antiperson mines, which in numerous countries compromise for a long time the return to peace . . . and which even long after the ceasing of hostilities, continue to kill and to cause irreparable damage" (Vatican Information Service [May 29, 1995]).

of tactical thought.[44] The phenomenon was not new; there had always been small-scale wars. What was new was the degree of clarity with which the superpowers analyzed and manipulated those conflicts as their pawns on a world scale, at the same time keeping them going and keeping them from escalating out of control.

In terms of just-war morality, low-intensity conflict is no easier to justify than larger wars. A conflict can drag on for years without a decision. High noncombatant casualties are unavoidable, proportionately higher than in battlefield war. The taking of hostages is routine. It is practically impossible for the supporting foreign powers to control the *in bello* tactics of their clients.[45] By the nature of the case, just-cause claims escape accountability to the local victim populations; in revolutionary settings, outside powers determine which government is legitimate on the grounds of its international connections or its ideology, appealing to imponderable values like "security" or "the Christian occident," or "liberation," which the intervening great powers claim to represent, thereby dressing local thugs in the trappings of moral causes. Since there can be no clearcut victory, the objective tends to descend to inflicting damage, or teaching a lesson, or proving one's resolution, thereby abandoning the discipline of the just-war criteria of intention, proportion, and probable success.

Humanitarian Intervention

The term *humanitarian intervention* was initially used to designate military operations undertaken in the interest of the people

---

[44]Loren B. Thomson treats the development of low-intensity conflict as an organic next step in the evolution of war (*Low-Intensity Conflict: The Pattern of Warfare* [Lexington, Mass.: Lexington Books, 1989]). Jack Nelson-Pallmeyer sees low-intensity conflict as a cynical way in which the great powers shift the suffering to surrogates in order to keep opposition from arising among their own people (*War Against the Poor* [Maryknoll, N.Y.: Orbis Books, 1989]).

[45]For the U.S. surrogate wars in Central America in recent decades, the CIA reportedly wrote manuals on assassinating government officials and training military personnel in torture techniques.

of a country against their own government, where the intervening power did not intend to annex or destroy the territory in question. In 1964 U.S. transport planes, with the help of Belgian paratroopers, extricated from major cities of Zaire foreign nationals stranded by that country's endemic chaos. In 1971 India intervened in the breakup of Pakistan, thereby assisting in the creation of an independent Bangladesh. In 1979 Tanzania intervened in Uganda to bring down the especially brutal dictatorship of Idi Amin and restore a semblance of legitimate government. More recently the same label was claimed for efforts to stabilize crises in Somalia and Rwanda, especially where efforts to serve refugees were being compromised by continuing military violence and banditry.

Sometimes the justification for such an intervention is claimed by a near neighbor, sometimes by a superpower. More recently there have been appeals to the United Nations or other regional authorities.

Peace Keeping

Since its origins the United Nations charter has authorized interposing armed but nonbelligerent forces along truce lines.[46] Some have been quite successful (Cyprus, the Sinai before 1967); in other settings, however, there is no peace to keep. Then the intervening force must choose between abandoning its mission and becoming one of the parties to the conflict.

Each of these modifications of the notion of justifiable war raises other questions. Which of the just-war criteria become especially weighty in each of these settings? Which of them become impossible to satisfy? Whatever conclusion nations and citizens come to will be better understood if seen in the light of the classical just-war grid.

---

[46]Larry L. Fabian, *Soldiers Without Enemies* (Washington, D.C.: The Brookings Institute, 1971); Indar Jit Rikhye, Michael Harbottle, and Bjørn Egge, *The Thin Blue Line: International Peacekeeping and Its Future* (New Haven: Yale University Press, 1974); A. B. Fetherston, *Towards a Theory of United Nations Peacekeeping* (New York: St. Martin's Press, 1994).

A Roman Catholic Response

In the spring of 1986, a few months before I came to the University of Notre Dame to teach social ethics and work with the staff of the Kroc Institute for International Peace Studies, I met with John Howard Yoder at a coffeehouse in Berkeley, California, where I then taught, to discuss my new responsibilities. Chief among his concerns was that I teach a course on military ethics organized principally for ROTC students.

Originally an interdisciplinary course generated in response to the Vietnam War, "War, Law, Ethics" had been taught by Yoder for several years. He felt that it would be appropriate for me, as a Catholic rooted in the just-war tradition, to conduct the course rather than himself, a Mennonite pacifist. Thus began one of the most fruitful teaching experiences in my career and one of the most nourishing intellectual dialogues of my lifetime. When I left Notre Dame a few years later, even after culling my files, I departed with three thick folders of Yoder's famous memos.

While I count my association with Professor Yoder as a privileged one, his influence on my generation of Catholic moral theologians has been profound. His witness as a theologian in the peace-church tradition is highly esteemed, and the seriousness with which he has carried out his role as a friendly critic of just-war thinking has without doubt contributed to sharpening its formulation and application in the American Catholic setting.

The acceptance given Yoder's thinking in Catholic circles, it must be said, owes something to the times. The Second Vatican

102

Council accelerated a reexamination of Catholic thinking on peace and the use of force begun with Pope John XXIII's *Pacem in terris*. The Council's ecumenism intensified interdenominational contacts and in the United States fostered interconfessional higher education. The Council's call for a renewal of moral theology placed high value on the use of biblical sources and on the Christian character of the people of God. The Vietnam War, the nuclear arms race, proxy wars in Central America, and finally the Gulf War brought bishops and theologians face to face with questions of war and peace. Finally, the pontificate of John Paul II has witnessed increasing support at the highest level for nonviolent resistance, especially in Eastern Europe, and for strict application of the just-war tradition, notably during the Gulf conflict.

Yoder's reputation among Catholic moralists, however, also owes a great deal to the integrity of his own theological vision and to the determination with which he has sought to engage just-war thinkers in serious dialogue. In the 1984 edition of *When War Is Unjust*, Yoder set four tests of the credibility of just-war thinking: (1) conceptual adequacy, (2) social or institutional capacity, (3) psychological conditions, and (4) moral responsiveness.

In contributing a Catholic commentary on Yoder's challenges, I would like to review developments in Roman Catholic thinking on the justifiable warfare tradition around the same four tests. In general, one may trace two main trends since World War II, but more especially in the quarter century since Vietnam, in the evolution of Catholic thinking on the ethics of force:

1) a narrowing of the gap between nonviolence and the just-war tradition, and

2) greater strictness in the application of just-war criteria to armed conflicts.

The following account, particularly of the *conceptual adequacy* of the official Catholic use of just-war thinking, I hope, will make those twin developments clear. At the same time, the growing lack of social conditions for authentic and effective use of the just-war analysis presents a challenge to all who would see themselves as adherents of a doctrine for the justifiable use of force.

Conceptual Adequacy:
Resistance to Evil and the Limited Use of Force

The test of *conceptual adequacy* raises three distinct issues:

1) the place of nonviolence in Catholic teaching and practice,

2) the problem of the sliding scale which allegedly prevents just-war criteria from having effective bite, and

3) the absence of public condemnation of unjust war.

The Role of Nonviolence

While there exists, at least since the rise of the modern nation-state, a broad Catholic peace tradition that includes nonviolence, the just-war tradition has been "in possession" in the Catholic community. The public teaching of the church and of Catholic theologians held that the church's ordinary teaching consisted of just-war doctrine. Nonviolence, equated with nonresisting pacifism, was either rejected or tolerated as a matter of personal conscience. Beginning with the Second Vatican Council, however, there has been increasing recognition of the value of nonviolence on the part of the official church.

The Council, having laid out a positive vision of peace, for the first time in the modern period affirmed the worth of nonviolence:

> We cannot fail to praise those who renounce the use of violence in the vindication of their rights and who resort to methods of defense which are otherwise available to weaker parties.[1]

The formulation is noteworthy in two respects. First, the Council affirms nonviolence as active resistance to evil. In conciliar teaching nonviolence is not a witness to be taken up for its own sake, but rather a preferred means for overcoming injustice.

---

[1] *Gaudium et spes* (*Pastoral Constitution on the Church in the Modern World*), no. 78, O'Brien and Shannon, *Catholic Social Thought: The Documentary Heritage.*

Second, contrariwise, nonviolence is not equivalent to non-resistance. In this sense, in the Catholic context, nonviolence shares with the just-war tradition a presumption that evil must be resisted, a conviction shared by leading nonviolent practitioners like Gandhi and King. In other words, "Peace must be pursued and rights defended within moral restraint and in the context of defining other basic human values."[2]

In the next stage in the recent evolution of official Catholic attitudes toward nonviolence, the U.S. bishops' 1983 pastoral letter *The Challenge of Peace* went further, affirming that nonviolence and the just-war tradition share "a complementary relationship," because, in their different ways, "each serves the common good" (par. 78).

In addition the two traditions share a common presumption against the use of force. In the case of nonviolence, aversion to the use of force itself is a value of decisive importance; in the just-war tradition, the avoidance of violence is rather a weighty value, which may be overridden in exceptional circumstances.

In their 1993 pastoral statement, *The Harvest of Justice Is Sown in Peace*, the bishops summarized their position this way:

1) In situations of conflict, our constant commitment ought to be, as far as possible, to strive for justice through nonviolent means.

2) But, when sustained attempts at nonviolent action fail to protect the innocent against fundamental injustice, then legitimate political authorities are permitted as a last resort to employ limited force to rescue the innocent and establish justice.[3]

Still, in the decade since *The Challenge of Peace* the official Catholic position on nonviolence has evolved in the direction of giving nonviolence standing as a public ethic by which to judge political institutions and public policy. *The Challenge of Peace* essentially regarded nonviolence as a personal vocation and just war as the state ethic. Ten years later, the bishops are bolder in proposing that nonviolence has a public role. *The Harvest of*

---

[2] National Conference of Catholic Bishops, *The Challenge of Peace*, no. 74.
[3] *The Harvest of Justice Is Sown in Peace: A Reflection of the National Conference of Catholic Bishops on the Tenth Anniversary of "The Challenge of Peace"* (Washington, D.C.: NCCB/USCC, 1993), 4. Henceforth, *HJSP.*

Justice Is Sown in Peace talks about a public obligation to support education and training in nonviolent means of defending justice, and it speaks of a duty of public officials to develop and utilize institutions which provide alternatives to the use of force (*HJSP*, 5).

The bishops' 1993 teaching was influenced by the role of nonviolence in world affairs in the ten years which had passed between the writing of the two documents. Nonviolent struggles in the Philippines, China, and Eastern Europe inspired confidence that nonviolence could be utilized on a mass scale even in totalitarian regimes to vindicate the rights of the people against unjust rulers. As Pope John Paul II wrote in the encyclical *Centesimus annus*, his personal commentary on the events in Eastern Europe:

> It seemed that the European order resulting from the Second World War and sanctioned by the Yalta Agreements could only be overturned by another war. Instead, it has been overcome by the nonviolent commitment of people who, while always refusing to yield to the force of power, succeeded time after time in finding effective ways of bearing witness to the truth.[4]

Further, in a rebuke of realist attitudes toward the use of force, he wrote, "These events [of 1989] are a warning to those who, in the name of political realism, wish to banish law and morality from the political arena." In his recent biography of the Holy Father, moreover, journalist Tad Szulc has shown the direct contribution Pope John Paul II made to a nonviolent transformation in Eastern Europe.[5]

Thus, while the conceptual foundations of Catholic teaching on the use of force have not changed—that there exists a right and an obligation to defend the common good and resist injustice—the relationship between nonviolence and just war has

---

[4] *Centesimus annus*, no. 23, in O'Brien and Shannon, *Catholic Social Thought*, 437-88.

[5] See Tad Szulc, *Pope John Paul II: The Biography* (New York: Scribner, 1995).

changed considerably over the past fifty years. From being a repressed part of the tradition, nonviolence has become "a complementary tradition" in the form of a personal or group vocation and from a personal vocation nonviolence in some respects has begun to emerge as a public duty. As a consequence, in contemporary Catholic teaching the threshold for justifiable war has been raised (*HJSP*, 5).

While some have speculated that it would be difficult to find a war that Pope John Paul II would find just, the Holy Father and the Holy See have been outspoken about the need for humanitarian intervention on the part of the international community in Bosnia. In his 1993 address to the diplomatic corps the Holy Father asserted that when "populations are succumbing to an unjust aggressor, states no longer have a 'right to indifference.' It seems clear that their duty is to disarm the aggressor, if all other means have proved ineffective."[6]

Applying this interpretation of humanitarian intervention to events in Bosnia in the summer of 1995, the papal nuncio to Bosnia, Archbishop Francesco Monterissi, after the fall of the United Nations safe haven of Srebrenica, argued, "The option of peace, dialogue and negotiation must be preferred 999 times out of a thousand. But when one is faced with a situation as serious as this one, and given the fact that repeated negotiations have not brought a positive outcome, one can also consider an intervention by the international community."[7]

Offsetting the Sliding Scale

John Yoder's critique of the conceptual adequacy of just-war thinking has less to do with its theological underpinnings than its ability to refine concepts sharply enough to make applications reliable in concrete circumstances of armed conflict.

The test of the sliding scale is a hard challenge to respond to because insofar as it is a tradition of teaching and casuistry, the

---

[6] John Paul II, "Address to the Diplomatic Corps," January 16, 1993, *Origins* 22:34 (February 4, 1993), 583-87.

[7] "Nuncio to Bosnia Calls for Limited, Decisive Military Intervention," *Catholic News Service* (July 19, 1995).

just-war tradition has normally worked in the realm of ideas, or what is benignly called public debate. Accordingly, there are bound to be disputes and different schools of thought, which make it difficult to arrive at definitive answers across a whole society. In addition, the evolution of warfare makes it exceedingly difficult for ethical formulations to keep up with the development of technologies of destruction, shifts in military strategy, and changes in the political context of warfare.

The nub of Yoder's friendly criticism of the conceptual inadequacy of just-war thinking, of course, is that "people who say they hold to such views have not begun to develop the tools to make them stick." At one level, the response is that as an ethical system the just war cannot be simply a dialogue between bishops and scholars. It must be part of a social system that helps make the norms of the system effective in changing political and social circumstances. This is the position of *The Harvest of Justice Is Sown in Peace*:

> In the absence of a commitment of respect for life and a culture of restraint, it will not be easy to apply the just-war tradition, not just as a set of ideas, but *as a system of effective social constraints on the use of force*. There is need for greater public understanding of just-war criteria and greater efforts to apply just-war restraints in political decision making and military planning, training and command systems, and public debate (*HJSP*, 6, emphasis added).

In addition, *The Harvest of Justice Is Sown in Peace* recognizes that just-war reasoning is not a matter of moral calculus, applying established principles to contemporary cases. Rather, right reasoning about matters of war and peace demands peaceful dispositions of restraint which are largely lacking in contemporary western society (*HJSP*, 6-7).

At another level, in response to the test of the sliding scale one may point to the church's teaching on just war as it applies to contemporary circumstances. In its conditional acceptance of deterrence, for example, *The Challenge of Peace* set standards of intent (deterrence only) and progressive disarmament that lay out serious baselines for public policy. Likewise, *The Harvest of*

Justice Is Sown in Peace offered refined statements of the just-war criteria that attempt to sharpen standards in light of prior omissions, changing military practice, and scholarly debate.

To deal with one of the more glaring omissions in the enforcement of just-war restraints, *The Harvest of Justice Is Sown in Peace* called for the application of just-war teaching to air combat, especially bombing doctrine (*HJSP*, 6). In response to the Gulf War strategy, it called into question the Powell doctrine of "overwhelming and decisive force" (*HJSP*, 6). In what was then virtually uncharted waters, it also applied just-war criteria to the conduct of the novel problem of humanitarian interventions (*HJSP*, 6). In the area of nuclear weapons, moving beyond the progressive disarmament criterion of *The Challenge of Peace*, *The Harvest of Justice Is Sown in Peace* calls for abolition of nuclear weapons as "a policy goal" (*HJSP*, 13).

Furthermore, based on the scholarly and professional debate of recent years, *The Harvest of Justice Is Sown in Peace* made a number of refinements in articulation of the just-war criteria; for example, clarifying the canon of success, so that it explicitly excludes both the excessive use of force (the realist temptation) and futile undertakings (the idealist delusion). Again, with respect to civilian immunity, *The Harvest of Justice Is Sown in Peace* attempts to deal with the erosion of respect for civilian life due to the military's increasing concern to avoid all casualties to its own personnel. It stipulates that even in cases where civilians may suffer accidentally, military personnel must take due care even at some risk to themselves (*HJSP*, 13).

So, on the test of conceptual adequacy, a Catholic rejoinder to Yoder is: (1) we take your point that more than public debate is necessary; to be effective just-war needs to be institutionalized in myriad ways; but (2) in terms of the refinement of norms and applications, whether in nuclear warfare, large-scale conventional warfare, or humanitarian intervention, the church's teaching has tried to match its principles to practical experience in ways which aim to make the just-war tradition applicable under contemporary military and political conditions.

Still, I have not answered Yoder's hardest question; namely, how is it that the tradition appears to fail to yield criticism of *unjust* war, especially where our own country is concerned?

The Hardest Question

To be sure, the style of the U.S. church has tended to be prospective. Relying on their role as moral teachers, the U.S. bishops have tended to raise questions about impending conflicts rather than issue condemnations after the fact. In the lead-up to the Gulf War, for example, Archbishop Roger Mahony's November 1990 letter on the Persian Gulf, endorsed by the body of bishops at their November 1990 meeting and later transmitted to President Bush by NCCB/USCC President Archbishop Daniel Pilarczyk, played an important role in defining the national debate generated by that conflict.[8]

Further, *The Harvest of Justice Is Sown in Peace* responded retrospectively. In 1993, after the Gulf War, it judged that the bombing of civilian infrastructure, the most morally problematic issue to arise from the Gulf War, "can amount to making war on noncombatants" (*HJSP*, 6). The bishops of the United States had, moreover, been frequent critics of U.S. policy in Central America during the 1980s, when they took a strict construction of just-war norms.[9] Pope John Paul II for his part was an unrelenting critic of the Gulf War, especially on grounds of last resort and proportionality, even though the U.S. media failed to cover his views. In the Holy Father's view, diplomatic efforts were never seriously tried.[10]

The major counter-example to the charge that just-war thinking fails to reach the bottom line of judging immoral acts of war or condemning unjust wars, of course, is the Vietnam War.

In 1968, at the height of U.S. involvement, in the pastoral letter *Human Life in Our Day*, the U.S. bishops raised questions

---

[8] "Mahony Letter on Just War Affirmed," *Origins* 20:24 (November 22, 1990), 384-86; Archbishop Daniel Pilarczyk, "Letter to President Bush: The Persian Gulf Crisis," *Origins* 20:25 (November 29, 1990), 397, 399-400.

[9] See Gerard Powers, "A Moral Critique of the Reagan Doctrine: A Case for Strictly Construing Just War Norms," in George A. Lopez and Drew Christiansen, *Morals and Might* (Boulder: Westview, 1995).

[10] See "John Paul II for Peace in the Middle East/War in the Gulf: Gleaning through the Pages of *L'Osservatore Romano*" (Vatican City: Libreria Editrice Vaticana, 1992).

about the proportionality of the war and defended the right to selective conscientious objection. Finally, in 1971 they called for an end to the war, saying:

> At this point in history it seems clear that whatever good we hope to achieve through continued involvement in this war is now outweighed by the destruction of human life and the moral values it inflicts. It is our firm conviction therefore that ending of this war is a moral obligation of the highest priority.[11]

Like many others, the U.S. Catholic bishops as a body came to their conclusion late in the conflict and did so on the basis of long-term judgments of proportionality.

There is an important lesson here for those who presume that moral judgments can be made instantaneously. For a great variety of reasons, it often takes time to sort out the morality or immorality of a military action. The *jus ad bellum* criteria, moreover, remain operative even during a war like Vietnam, and judgments can change in the light of new information or greater experience. Where the grounds (among others) for opposing a war have to do with proportion, for example, one needs to expect that wars that at an early stage might be seen as just may be judged unjust later, as evidence of disproportion mounts.

Still, the grounds for the U.S. bishops' judgment in 1971, like so many before them, were just-war grounds.[12] Indeed, many critics of the war, if they did not discover the just-war tradition in formulating the criticism, were forced to reinvent it, giving proof to John Courtney Murray's maxim about "the eternal return of the natural law," by which he referred to the just-war tradition.

Thus, where there is extended debate, as in the case of Vietnam in the late 1960s and early 1970s, of nuclear warfare in the

---

[11] "Resolution on Southeast Asia" (Washington, D.C.: NCCB/USCC, 1971).

[12] On episcopal response to the Vietnam War, see David J. O'Brien, "American Catholic Opposition to the Vietnam War: A Preliminary Assessment," in Shannon, *War or Peace?*, 119-50, esp. 124-31.

1980s, or the Gulf War in the 1990s, the just-war tradition as applied by the church and countless millions of people can lead to hard judgments that acts of war and particular wars are unjust. So, to the test of conceptual adequacy, one may respond:

1) The clarification of the conceptual foundations of the just-war tradition—resistance to evil by nonviolent means if possible, by limited use of force if necessary—has raised the threshold for resort to the use of force;

2) Recent applications of the just-war tradition in the Catholic church have attempted to tighten the criteria for a justifiable conflict, and

3) The just-war tradition has served as the basis for critique of military policies and opposition to war.

Social or Institutional Capacity

Yoder's second test has to do with the capacity of a society to avoid the use of force and restrain its use. *The Harvest of Justice Is Sown in Peace* gave a partial answer to this question. It recommended, as we have seen, national programs in nonviolent education and training. In addition, it proposed that "new styles of preventative diplomacy and conflict resolution ought to be explored, tried, improved and supported" (*HJSP*, 5). It noted, moreover, that the availability of such techniques "raises the threshold for the recourse to force."

A full reply to the test of institutional capacity requires, however, that we take Yoder's point. Whether in the area of alternative means of conflict resolution or in application of just-war criteria to potential uses of force, for the most part the United States today lacks the social and institutional capacity to utilize alternatives to the use of force or to effect adherence to just-war norms in times of conflict.

A particularly serious gap is any lack of provision under U.S. law for selective conscientious objection, that is, objection to military service in particular circumstances because of a conscientious judgment that a given war or military action is contrary to just-war norms. The Catholic church in the United States has long sought such protection as a corollary to the acceptance of the just-war tradition (*HJSP*, 7).

Simply put, if it is morally permissible and even obligatory to engage in a just war, then it is morally impermissible to participate in an unjust one and one would be morally required to refuse to serve under such conditions.

The failure of the military to revise its own regulations to process selective conscientious objectors, and of the Congress to allow for selective objection on just-war grounds continues to put those who adhere to the just-war tradition in jeopardy. While the issue is complicated by the present volunteer status of today's military, the lack of effective remedies for selective conscientious objectors remains a problem both for personal conscience and for the development of just-war thinking as an effective system of social constraints on the immoral use of force.

Psychological Conditions

Yoder asks, "What are the *psychological* requisites for the criteria to operate? What kinds of people are ready to make judgments independent of the authorities? How do we produce such people?"

Independence of mind, I believe, is only one of the psychological conditions for making the just-war criteria effective, and one whose importance, especially in the context of American rugged individualism, is easily overestimated. I would submit that opposition to authority will rightly emerge when the other moral virtues necessary for making judgments on the use of force, such as respect for life, moderation, restraint, and prudence are present. It is the whole weight of one's moral character, rather than the readiness to resist alone, which will prepare a person conscientiously to object to an unjust use of force. On the issue of character, I would submit, proponents of nonviolence and the adherents of the just-war tradition should share a common agenda.

The Harvest of Justice Is Sown in Peace warns that the social psychological conditions for application of the just-war criteria are seriously lacking in contemporary society.

Moral reflection on the use of force calls for a spirit of moderation rare in contemporary political culture. The increasing violence of our society, its growing insensitivity to the sacredness of life and the glorification of the technology of destruction in popular culture could inevitably impair our society's ability to apply just-war criteria in time of crisis (*HJSP*, 6).

In a culture of violence, to be sure, the uses of the just-war tradition can easily degenerate into "a weapon to justify a political conclusion or a set of mechanical criteria that automatically yields a simple answer" quite inconsistent with the underlying intention of the tradition to prevent conflict and to discern the moral limits of justifiable force.

When one weighs the so-called technological imperative, the inertial force of political and military bureaucracies along with the growing brutalization of culture cited by the U.S. bishops, Yoder has good reason to wonder whether the social psychological conditions to make the just-war system effective in bringing about social constraints against the immoral use of force are available today.

Moral Responsibility

Under the title of *moral responsibility* Yoder addresses principally the risks and sacrifices that must be undertaken by the individuals and groups who oppose or refuse to participate in a war or action they judge to be unjust.

To be fair, one must say that risks and sacrifices of a grave sort are borne by those in the military services who judge a war to be just and so find themselves duty-bound to defend the innocent and uphold justice by military means. Catholic teaching affirms that "a citizen may not casually disregard his country's conscientious decision to call its citizens to legitimate acts of defense" (*HJSP*, 7).

At the same time, the teaching maintains that "no state may demand blind obedience." Accordingly, as we have seen, the church in the United States has actively supported legal protection for those who conscientiously refuse to participate in any war (conscientious objectors) as well as for those who cannot, in good conscience, serve in specific conflicts they consider unjust or in branches of the service (e.g., strategic nuclear forces) which are required to carry out morally repugnant policies (indiscriminate killing).

According to *The Harvest of Justice Is Sown in Peace*, especially in the case of compulsory military service, conscientious objectors ought to be ready to carry out alternative service to the community. The case of selective conscientious objectors in a volunteer military is more complex. "Individual objectors must exercise their rights in a responsible way," the 1993 pastoral statement says, "and there must be reliable procedures to verify the validity of their claims" (*HJSP*, 7).

In practice, some objection will be to specific actions which already have the weight of military law against them (for example, an order to engage in torture or rape). Such objection is protected under military law, and while disobedience to an illegal order is difficult to execute, probably entailing some sacrifice for a subordinate, the weight of the law will be with the objector.

In other cases—for example, strategic bombing—the offense may be all the graver, but unfortunately the law will offer no support. In practice, the military may prefer to dismiss an objector from the service or reassign the individual rather than bring more serious legal action. Again, there will be a price to pay for conscientious action, but frequently not the grave price that might have been paid at another time under different conditions.

Because of their position, today's military conscientious objectors risk losing the good opinion of others and may encounter disagreeable bureaucratic haggling, abuse from colleagues and superiors, and some serious inconveniences, such as reimbursing college expenses. These are far less extreme penalties than the prison sentences meted out to objectors in the past.

If those who directly execute military policy must be ready to pay the price of conscience, greater responsibility must also be shown by political leaders, civilian officials, and policy-makers, as well as the military high command. Resignation in protest, to be sure, is neither the only nor the surest way to correct an immoral policy, but the low incidence of protest by officials who retire in times of crisis sets a poor precedent for critique and correction of morally flawed policies.

In sum, civilian leaders and officials, like military personnel, should be prepared to bear the onus of selective conscientious objection. While the price one may pay today is not as heavy as it once was, the effectiveness of the just-war tradition as a system of moral constraints on the use of force depends very much on the willingness of conscientious men and women to pay a price for their moral convictions.

By the same token, I would insist that *resistance* (and civil disobedience) itself should not be the goal. The tradition of civil disobedience in America has been badly tarnished by too great a willingness to resist or, perhaps, appear to be a resister. Objection to unjust war must grow out of a broad set of ethical commitments, virtues, and dispositions, which lead one to protest the immoral use of force in which moral discrimination and respect for one's adversary have an important place.

Summary

When War Is Unjust continues to provide thoughtful challenges to the integrity of just-war thinking. I have endeavored to show that, as moral teaching, contemporary Catholic teaching meets Yoder's challenge on several counts.

While church teaching remains influential, it does not carry the weight it once may have had. There is a pluralism—one hesitates to say fragmentation—of moral authority in contemporary American society. Just-war thinking is broadly shared by a host of professions including law and philosophy. The multiplicity of sources of moral authority makes it difficult to arrive at a societal consensus on the meaning of the just-war canons and their application.

In addition, the academic venue of a great deal of debate, while it can contribute to the clarity on the issues, may lack commitment to the underlying values of just-war thinking (the pursuit of justice and the avoidance of violence) and the practical, pastoral concern for the integrity and responsibility of conscience that attended the use of the tradition in a church context. Furthermore, as at all times, the application of just-war thinking is subject to ideological distortion. In a pragmatic culture like ours, which puts a premium on a superficial contest of ideas, there is good reason to suspect facile judgments claiming the authority of the tradition.

Finally, we must concede that the social and psychological conditions for making just-war reasoning effective as a system of social constraints are lacking. The absence of protection for selective conscientious objection is a major deficiency, but to that must be added (among others) the lack of accountability of air power, the absence of the habit of resignation in protest, and the need in public institutions for conflict resolution and training in nonviolence.

So, while in the main church teaching has met many of the tests Yoder sets for the just-war tradition as a system of ideas, as a system of social constraints on the use of force it remains a weak social force. As the U.S. bishops wrote in 1993:

> Ten years after *The Challenge of Peace*, given the neglect of the peaceable virtues and the destructiveness of today's weaponry, serious questions remain about whether modern war in all its savagery can meet the hard test set by the just war tradition (*HJSP*, 6).

DREW CHRISTIANSEN, S.J.
United States Catholic Conference
Washington, D.C.

APPENDIX I

The State of the Question

THE STATE OF THE QUESTION: Analysis of the validity of the just-war tradition, as a morally accountable position, when seen from the perspective of careful ethical method.

A. FORMULATING THE STATE OF THE ISSUE: How does one evaluate the global adequacy of a system of moral discourse?

1. The just-war tradition represents not a simple body of rules, but a global stance within which the detailed applications continue to evolve. The continuing change is, however, not such as to prevent our considering it a consistent system. It does have in principle a kind of logical coherence.

2. The relative restraints represented by the just-war tradition represent a degree of respect for the initial Christian rejection of all war. Once war is contemplated, it must bear the burden of proof in the face of the negative presumption that war is always materially evil (that is, harmful) and often morally wrong. The various criteria of the just-war tradition are intended to safeguard the prima facie rights of others not to be harmed, or the duty not to harm others.[1]

3. The just-war tradition can be morally respectable if and when it implements a critique of the "anything goes" approach to war, variously described as Machiavellianism, *raison d'etat*, divine right, national interest, realism, or fascism.

---

[1] See Childress, "Just War Criteria."

119

    a. There are real people who do take such positions, denying any real moral restraint. They are not a hypothetical construct. It is important to resist them. If applied with integrity, the just-war tradition will/would resist them.

    b. These are not moral positions, whether that be measured by the philosophical criteria for a moral point of view, by the actual demands and interests of the rest of the world community, or by Christian morality.

    c. The phrases *divine right* and *national interest* can in some special contexts be given a less irresponsible meaning than the above. *Divine right* can mean that a ruler is morally accountable. Valid *national interest* can be so defined as not to be a blank check but to set limits.

    d. The just-war tradition avoids the errors of national interest by stating criteria independent of the given State's perspective and interest.

4. The just-war tradition is morally preferable to the holy war or the crusade view, in which appeal to the transcendent value of one's own cause decreases or denies the restraints imposed by the rights of the adversary or of the innocent.

    a. There are people who take such positions. They claim a transcendent mandate which is held to overrule not only the rights of the adversaries and neutrals, but even prudence in the costs inflicted on one's own population. Our freshest example is the Ayatollah.

    b. Such views also fall short of the normal criteria for a moral position (as in 3b above).

    c. The just-war tradition corrects for this error by naming several distinct empirical criteria, applied to the concrete facts of the case, without concern for transcendent authority.

5. The just-war tradition is morally credible if and as it rejects the several forms of irrational and romantic glorification of honor, the nation, courage, or militant virility.

    a. There are people who do take such positions. Sylvester Stallone makes millions from it. It is a part of basic military training in some services in some countries. It is part of the militant national myth of peoples who have had to come to terms with defeat: Masada, the Warsaw ghetto, Polish romanticism, "Remember the Alamo." Michael Walzer calls it "frenzy" or "excess killing."

    b. Evidently this is not a moral position, though those who adopt it may at the outset lay some claim to just cause, or manliness, courage, or honor as a virtue. It certainly does serve as ground in real life for assigning praise and blame. It respects none of the standard criteria.

6. The moral credibility of the just-war tradition will therefore be contingent upon its effectively exercising those restraints which distinguish it theoretically from the holy war, from "anything goes," and from Rambo. Though those three types differ logically, they may flow into one another, and the restraint they call for would be the same.

7. Long-range moral credibility on the part of persons or institutions holding to the just-war tradition will therefore be contingent upon clarification of their resources to implement those restraints, especially:
    a. Clarifying the doctrine so that its application is less arbitrary, more objective, more nearly automatic.
    b. Teaching the doctrines so that responsible individuals (Christians, citizens, legislators, soldiers) will know of their duty to refuse to execute unjust orders or to vote for or to serve in unjust wars.
    c. Making alternative plans for the non-military defense of social values in situations where those values can no longer legitimately be defended militarily.
    d. Encouraging agencies of moral insight (church hierarchies, journalistic and educational institutions, research agencies) to commit to provide the factual data that will enable independent judgment regarding the justice of certain causes and the usability of certain weapons. There cannot be a responsible independent moral judgment without having credible nonestablishment sources of information.

8. Who needs to be convinced that a given war is justified?
    a. The ecumenical challenge comes from those who doubt that the just-war tradition is in fact an instrument of moral discernment.
       i. This may be challenged on systematic grounds; the doctrine is so complex, so multifactored, so ill-defined that it cannot be effectively applied.

      ii. The claim may be historical; the system could theoretically have worked, but those who say that they hold to it do not in fact apply it.

      iii. The claim may be moral; it may be held that those who say they hold to it do not in fact show that they intend to apply it.

    b. The practical challenge comes from the other side. The common-sense criterion is the perspective of the people in the "enemy" nation. Reversibility is a standard moral concept.

B. THE FURTHER AGENDA IF THE TRADITION IS TO BECOME CREDIBLE. The clarification of the doctrine (called for by item 7a above) will need to plug these gaps where the traditional doctrine has been left irresponsibly open-ended:

1. The interface of *in bello* with *ad bellum*: When does a war become no longer valid because the only available means of pursuing it are illegitimate?

    a. The appeal to necessity is a frequent cover for this gap. A valid just-war reasoning process will not use the concept of necessity in such a loose way. That the means are necessary—the end cannot be reached without them—is an indispensable but not a sufficient criterion. It does not justify setting aside the other criteria.

    b. The use of illegitimate means may not disqualify the cause, but it may undercut the claim to be a just authority. Where does that line run? We tend to apply it quickly to the adversary.[2]

2. The notion of last resort would be radically changed if serious attention were given to available or conceivable non-military and/or nonviolent means of defending the values which are at stake.[3]

3. The redefinition of *innocence*. Etymologically and legally, *innocent* meant "making no threat." It was originally a statement

---

[2] In fact, sometimes the enemy's *in bello* abuses, usually called atrocities, are the decisive basis for a just-cause claim against that enemy. This is one place where people reason asymmetrically. When the *in bello* infractions are committed on our side, they are called excesses or unintentional or collateral, and it is argued that they do not compromise our cause.

[3] *The Challenge of Peace* and *The Harvest of Justice Is Sown in Peace* recognize this connection, as do some academics, but no such recognition seems to matter in public life.

about whether the person was harmful, not about morality or guilt. It applied even to the off-duty soldier. The concept has been irresponsibly whittled away:

a. by the idea that all who contribute to the economic or moral solidarity of the enemy are fair targets, for example, the "quasi-combatant work force";

b. by the idea that enemy civilians are responsible for the wrong actions of their governments because they should have stopped them (although most enemy nations are not democracies, and although even in Western democracies the civilians have little share in the decision to go to war and still less to say about how it is waged);

c. by the idea that "enemy" civilians, even if unarmed, are not innocent if they are patriotic;

d. by the theories described as "fortress" or "siege" or "fish in the sea," declaring innocent lives to be forfeited because of the proximity of soldiers;

e. by guerrilla tactics which cannot respect the classical demands for belligerent ethics (wearing the uniform, displaying weapons) in the face of governments which refuse to recognize their belligerent status;

f. by "lowering the hurdle"; for example, removing those restraining rules one believes will not be respected in any case, with the justification that respect for law is weakened by having rules that will not be kept;

g. by not accepting surrender (this used to be called refusing quarter). In the last days of the Gulf War, fleeing combatants were gunned down on the road or bulldozed over in their trenches with no way for them to surrender, partly on the ground of the fear that a fleeing ex-combatant is a future combatant.[4]

4. The general drift of the evolution of military practice (as distinct from the just-war tradition theoretical level and from the specifics named in the international treaties) has been to permit more and more violence and to limit progressively the realm of immunity as the technology has evolved. Though never stated as *intending* to abandon *all* restraint, the real capacity to restrain has been constantly losing ground. What has been permitted has

---

[4] In the particular case of Iraqis fleeing Kuwait, the stated war aim of freeing Kuwait had already been achieved before the massacre on the road to Basra.

become increasingly destructive, as what is forbidden is pushed back on the scale.[5] Technology has escalated faster than treaties to discipline its use can keep up. If the just-war tradition is to be made credible it will need to be seen at some point to be gaining ground in defining restraints rather than constantly giving ground in order to be "realistic."

5. Specimens of the needed "firming up" which has been taking place modestly and which may point toward such a partial restoration of credibility, have been:
    a. nuclear pacifism;
    b. war crimes trials;
    c. Vietnam selective objection;
    d. continuing low-key work at the United Nations on drafting additional conventions;
    e. growing citizen responsibility.

C. PROPORTIONAL REASONING: HOW CAN IT BE VALID?

1. There must be some effort to make serious the language of proportionality, i.e. of evils being measured as "greater" and "lesser." Those who use it claim implicitly that quasi-quantifiable evaluations of the several costs and benefits at stake can be made, yet often the claim is not supported by providing any responsible definitions. How can one claim to weigh:
    • combatant lives against non-combatant lives?
    • lives against freedom or the danger of anarchy?
    • future genetic damage against present political interest?
    • the additional jeopardy to combatants which may result from not targeting churches, libraries, museums, thereby making it harder to sweep into control of a city?
    • the lives of civilians in an enemy country against those of our country or the rest of the world?
    Can there possibly be clear "coefficients" for weighing different kinds of damage against one another?

2. Proportionality estimation must take into account not only the specific destruction one contemplates just now, but also of the

---

[5] See chapter 5, the section entitled "The Scale Keeps Sliding," pages 50-67 above. Such escalation beyond the original justification is exemplified by the bombing of Baghdad in 1991, the bombing of Hanoi in 1972, the massive city bombings in Germany in 1944-45, where the destruction was not related in any disciplined way to the achievement of the stated war goals.

probability of escalation. The party provoking the escalation, by taking action likely to trigger that response, must somehow share responsibility for the increased danger and damage.

3. Consequential estimations must take into account the probability of error in factual readings and predictions. The more variables there are, the more actors there are, the greater the chances that we will be killing people and crushing cultures on the basis of mistaken information. If a particular calculation of empirical facts and/or probable consequences depends upon four fallible factual readings, and each of those four readings has an accuracy probability of 80 percent, then the chance that the ultimate prediction, on the basis of which the decision is justified, will be accurate is 41 percent, hardly a strong moral basis for evaluating action on the basis of outcomes.

4. Consequential calculations are challenged in principle, from some classical moral perspectives, by some serious thinkers, as an intrinsically unworthy moral stance. They tend to reduce fellow human beings to means to one's own ends, unless the consequences *for everyone* are in the calculation. But even for those who do consider consequential or proportionate reasoning to be acceptable in principle, the ways in which it calculates must be accountable, and the alternatives to inflicting what one holds to be a greater evil must be thought about seriously. This critique is strengthened, of course, when one party is judge, jury, prosecutor, and executioner in the case.

D. INSTITUTIONAL REQUISITES for the application of the criteria to be a serious possibility[6]:

1. The application of the criteria is impossible if there is not an educational program which enables a population and its decision-makers to share an informed understanding of the criteria. Currently the existence of such educational resources is a rare

---

[6] For this entire section see John Howard Yoder, "The Credibility and Political Uses of the Just War Tradition," in Lopez and Christiansen, *Morals and Might* (also available from the Joan B. Kroc Institute for International Peace Studies, Notre Dame, IN 46556 [working paper 1:C{ED}:12]); and idem, "The Credibility of Ecclesiastical Teaching on the Morality of War," in *Celebrating Peace*, ed. Leroy S. Rouner (Notre Dame, Ind.: University of Notre Dame Press, 1990), 33-51.

exception. This lacuna would need to be met in different forms on different levels: Christian catechesis, the citizenry as a whole, and military personnel.

2. The application of the criteria is impossible if there is not a source of information about the facts of each case. Just-war discrimination (as distinguished from the other views) is based upon the empirical data needed to measure just cause and last resort, which are matters of political fact, and to measure discrimination and proportion, which are matters of technology, skill, and operating procedures. All of these empirical readings add up to a verdict on probable success. The governing authorities cannot be expected to provide objective information on these matters, which might call into question their intentions. Any bona fide intention to respect the just-war discipline will therefore demand independent fact-finding. Only to a very limited degree do the media even in the most free societies provide such information.

3. The application of the criteria is not serious if the discerning of limits is left to the integrity of individual impulse and heroic conscientiousness. Resistance to unjust orders or selective objection will fall apart under divide-and-conquer pressures of the authorities if the discernment and the refusal to serve are not concerted. That demands agencies of shared decision.[7]

4. The readiness to apply the criteria is not serious if there has been no attention to what it would be proper for a community to do when a war *cannot* be prosecuted legally or morally. The notion of last resort is not being applied honestly if there are no plans made for the conditions under which it would be morally right to sue for peace.[8] This requirement applies both to the war as a

---

[7] It would in fact be far more credible if this decision were illuminated by perspectives beyond those of the parties to the conflict. This is why the British diplomat David Urquhart proposed to the First Vatican Council that it should set up an agency to evaluate wars for their conformity to the law of nations (see "David Urquhart and the Challenge of 'Just War' at Vatican I" available from the Joan B. Kroc Institute for International Peace Studies, Notre Dame, IN 46556 [working paper 3:WP:8]). World Order visions developing from the Middle Ages to the United Nations were driven by this idealism.

[8] See Yoder, "Surrender: A Moral Imperative," and the statement of the same concern by John Courtney Murray, S.J. in "Remarks on the Moral Problem of War."

whole and to discerning when a specific command should be disobeyed.

5. Still more complex than being serious about the limits of legitimacy is the imperative of providing alternative means of defending a community's values.

   a. There would be legitimate military means which might still be used without resort to the illegitimate ones.

   b. There would be nonviolent means, like those which have occasionally been resorted to spontaneously in response to oppression.[9]

   c. There should be recognition of the far greater possibilities which would obtain if such nonviolent means were trained for (as are military means), interpreted in historical context, and related to the cultural virtues of the nation.[10]

Only when such alternative recourses have been seriously thought about can they count as part of the evaluation of last resort. And only if they have been made the object of contingency thinking, in the same order of seriousness applied to advance planning for the wise use of justified military means, can we claim to have thought seriously about them.

E. TRIAL BALANCE PENDING FURTHER EVIDENCE

The clarifications projected in this outline belong to the integrity of the just-war tradition claim. They are not mere debating points made by pacifists or "realists" against the just-war tradition. They are the conditions of its credibility from within. They are intended to give the just-war tradition the benefit of the doubt. To sum up:

---

[9] See the section of the bibliography entitled "Selective Bibliography on Nonviolent Defense Alternatives," pages 165f. below.

[10] "In the past, most nonviolent struggles have been improvised, without large-scale preparation or training. Thus they may be simply prototypes of what could be developed by deliberate efforts" (Gene Sharp, Foreword to *People Power: The Philippine Revolution of 1986* [Manila: Reuter, 1986]). We would not think to ask that military means be evaluated by what they could achieve without theorizing, training, and equipment, yet nonviolence is often found wanting a priori by people who observe the limits of what it achieves when its use is spontaneous and sporadic (see Yoder, "The Power of Nonviolence").

1. Historical experience gives us few heartening examples of the tradition's "working" to provide clear restraint.

2. In the absence of the significant solidification called for in A6 and A7, and in B and C above, the consistent moral theologian must regretfully conclude that the just-war tradition has not yet established its moral credibility. In practice the just-war tradition most often serves:

   a. as a screen for behavior which is really less moral than the doctrine calls for, because after the theologians have promised something more discriminating, what really occurs is according to the holy-war or Rambo or anything-goes logic; or

   b. as rhetoric for the political opposition; or

   c. as rhetoric for the other side, which does not have access to particular kinds of power and weapons. The other side can use just-war criteria to condemn use of illegitimate power and weapons as unjust, even if it might use them if it had them.

3. The careful ethicist will continue to respect, and will desire to enhance, efforts being made to bring laws, treaties, and actual military practice more nearly in line with the just-war restraints. Inadequate as they are, they include:

   a. any rejection of indiscriminate bombing or shelling;

   b. any defense of the immunity of the innocent and of third parties, not only against direct attack but against hostage-taking, reprisals, and indirect attack;

   c. any defense of the dignity of individuals against inhumane conditions of detention or torture;

   d. any concern of military educators and command hierarchies to strengthen the readiness of their subordinates to refuse unjust orders and to reward those who respect the rights of adversaries and the innocent;

   e. any way to limit the "anything goes" or "no substitute for victory" use of the concept of necessity.

The above questions are dictated by the ground rules of ethics as an intellectual discipline. They will be asked by anyone concerned for honest moral reasoning, whatever such person's own orientation might be:

realist, pacifist, crusading, virtuous, honorable, or neutral/objective. They are most at home within serious application of the just-war framework. They are *not* derived from or dependent on a specifically Christian or specifically pacifist orientation; such commitments would add yet other questions to the list.

How War Becomes/Became Total

The notion of total war is widely used but seldom clearly defined. It always has something to do with going beyond limits, but the ways in which that happens are often not analyzed critically.[1] It will be helpful if we seek to itemize and disentangle the varieties of ways in which war, by becoming total, can break out of the restraints of the just-war tradition:

I. What one claims as *just cause* (or objective intention) may become total.

   A. The concept of unconditional surrender, as proclaimed by the Allies in World War II denies that war's goals can be limited. It thereby denies to the enemy any conditions under which to sue for peace.

   B. Under the heading of supreme emergency one can claim that civilization itself, or freedom, or the rule of law is at stake, in some absolute sense, and not merely the survival of a particular government. This may be held to justify actions, like city bombings, which would otherwise be wrong.[2]

---

[1] Raymond Aron gives no one definition of what makes war "total" (*The Century of Total War* [Garden City: Doubleday, 1954]). Thomas Powers and Ruthven Fremain likewise provide no one definition (*Total War: What It Is, How It Got That Way* [N.Y. Morrow, 1988]).

[2] See Walzer, *Just and Unjust Wars*, 225 ff.; Johnson, *The Just War Tradition and the Restraints of War* (Princeton, N.J.: Princeton University Press, 1981), 74, 237.

C. Any civil war is total as to cause, from the side of the government, in that the enemy has no right to exist. This was the case for the Union position in the Civil War in the United States (1861-65). The Confederate cause, on the other hand, was *not* total, in that (unlike an insurrection which seeks to take over the whole nation) the South sought only to secede.

D. Any *ideological* cause is by implication intrinsically uncompromising. One would rather die than settle for less than total victory. Revolution is the most common of these, but defense of freedom or socialism can also be made absolute.

1. *Empire* is by its nature an unlimited cause.
2. Machiavellian *raison d'état* or the theory of realism denies any restraints except the limits of a State's power.
3. The notion of national sovereignty as an absolute makes this claim in principle, whatever be the cause at stake.
4. Fascism as a theory raises the claim to the level of a right or duty to reject any limitations on the state's claims.
5. The rhetoric of holy war resurfaces when a government wants to mobilize mass support.

E. The political objective may escalate from defense against attack to the annihilation of the enemy (genocide) or of the enemy government (unconditional surrender). "Carthage is to be destroyed" was Rome's slogan in the Punic Wars. There is then no way for the enemy to sue for peace before total collapse. For example, the stated goals of World War II against the Axis escalated when at Casablanca President Roosevelt announced unconditional surrender as the war goal. The stated goals of the war against Iraq escalated after hostilities began in January 1991.

F. Racist or culturally ethnocentric convictions regarding the lesser dignity of other kinds of people may be used to justify respecting the rights, claims, and dignity of the enemy less. This has, of course, often been the case in colonial settings.

G. The above forms of escalation are not clearly different from *authority* becoming total. Marxism or Fascism or freedom or anti-communist "national security" can also be made absolute in a metaphysical way such as to be subject to no restraint. This can be thought of as inhering in the cause, but it can also be claimed as unique validation for the special claims of the State. The rise of democracy since the eighteenth century may lead to the citizens' being told that they have a greater stake in the nation than before, and therefore less reason to be critical. In any case, popularization or demagoguery decreases the possibility that wise diplomatic elites might save the peace by compromise.

H. *Totalitarianism* as a concept describes a kind of government as a whole. The term was at first used favorably to describe Mussolini. It is marked by dictatorship, absolutizing the nation-state over against other communities, internal policing directed to all of the citizenry, prohibition of dissent, and the suspension of individual rights.[3] All of these changes decrease the room for any notion of restraint in foreign relations.

II. *Means* may become total.

A. Certain weapons are intrinsically indiscriminate, not only massive explosives but also bacteriological and chemical weapons in air or water. Conventional weapons can also be used so as to deny restraint. The fire-bombings of Hamburg, Dresden, Tokyo, and other places were no less total than the nuclear attack on Hiroshima.

B. The speed of troop movements and (even more) of weapons delivery makes it nearly impossible to control escalation, weakening such traditional restraints as the cooling-off period and time for diplomats to work, and thereby decreasing the likelihood of other recourses prior to "last resort."

C. The vulnerability of command and communications makes it nearly impossible to control escalation. Preprogrammed retaliation may be impossible to call back.

D. A weapons system may take on an uncontrollable institutional momentum; for example, once it was decided to produce

---

[3] See Anthony Giddens, *The Nation State and Violence* (Berkeley: University of California, 1987); José Comblin, *The Church and the National Security State* (Maryknoll, N.Y.: Orbis Books, 1979), 64-81.

the atomic bomb, there was never a serious question about whether to use it.

E. The risk of a surprise attack (with its inherent tactical advantages) and the pervasive belligerent mentality ("cold war") may make a state of war quasi-permanent, eliminating the original understanding that the distance between peace and war is a high threshold to be crossed only very deliberately.

F. The social processes of mobilization, propaganda, and journalism normally have an escalatory impact. They tend to increase the population's readiness to accept decisions once implemented, and to decrease a government's ability to exercise moderation. As a war drags on, because of the need to hold the nation together, it tends to escalate from "justifiable" to "holy." This happened to the United States in 1861-65 and 1916-18. (This fact also belongs under IIIA below.)

G. Political interests drive belligerents into alliances which decrease each party's freedom to maneuver. Joining Clemenceau in order to defeat the Kaiser in World War I made it impossible for President Wilson to achieve some of his stated war aims. Joining Stalin in order to defeat Hitler made it impossible for the Allies to achieve the initially stated war aims.

H. A fanatical ruler when losing may command the destruction of his own civilization in order to deprive the enemy of the pleasure of winning; for example, Hitler decreeing "scorched earth," Sadam Hussein burning the Kuwaiti oil fields.

I. When the adversary's strength is so great that there is no chance of winning within ordinary limits, then some advocate the legitimacy of disregarding *some* of the rules. This is argued in "liberation" contexts on behalf of guerrilla or irregular forces, or of terrorism. It is argued in the nuclear debate against fully respecting innocent immunity.

III. *Combatant status* may become total.

A. Economic integration means that every productive worker can be considered an enemy. One speaks of the work force as "quasi-combatant." This is, of course, never *really* true of the old, the ill, infants. In no case does participating in the wartime economy remove most civilians from what *innocent* used to mean; namely, doing no direct military harm.

B. Universal military service makes everyone potentially a soldier.

C. Ideological reasons given for combat may make everyone on the other side psychologically an enemy.

D. The component of morale in contributing to social efficiency may make terror an effective weapon. This was the argument of Arthur ("Bomber") Harris of England in favor of the indiscriminate bombing of German cities in World War II.[4] For some, the component of a high level of popular support for a war, created by propaganda, is a mark of totalization; everyone is then a legitimate target.

E. Democracy makes everyone a responsible part of the legitimate authority waging the war (assuming an ideal view of democracy).

F. Involving the entire population, mostly unlearned, in the decision-making process makes room for demagoguery and abandons the restraint for which aristocrats of greater civility would be concerned.

> Restricted warfare was one of the loftiest achievements of the eighteenth century. It belongs to the class of hothouseplants which can only thrive in an aristocratic and qualitative civilisation.[5]

G. In sum, with regard to the enemy population, the effect of the phenomenon of "totalization" as a whole is to shrink the category of the non-combatant. With regard to "our" population, it may tend to increase the moral solidarity of the individual

---

[4] Walzer, *Just and Unjust Wars*, 258-61, 323-25.
[5] Guglielmo Ferrero, *Peace and War* (Freeport, N.Y.: Books for Libraries, 1969; original 1933).

citizen with what the government says it is doing for the cause of the people.

IV. *Last resort* may become an empty set. Even in peacetime military readiness may be held at such a pitch that there can be no real decision at any one point about whether to go to war (IIE above). The place of the military in administering the peacetime society and economy (e.g., in the national security state ideology [see IH above]) renders null the notion of any transition from peace to war.

Why Should We Keep the Rules *in Bello*?

A Mental Exercise and Study Aid

How rules are kept, and how faithfully they are kept, depends partly on why they are being kept and who is keeping them. The reasons for keeping them which have counted in past experience with the just-war tradition have been quite diverse, even though people are seldom self-conscious about those differences. That is why this exercise is needed. This variety will have quite diverse implications as to how the rules will work cross-culturally or how they may be respected in a society undergoing rapid value change. Failure to discern the variety of modes of argument and decision may lead not only to misunderstanding but also to moral failure.

The varied formulations that follow may sometimes appear to be nearly parallel or to overlap, yet they differ logically in important ways.[1]

All of the positions described assume that the *content* of the rules *in bello* (i.e., which particular actions or intentions are forbidden or commanded) have been and can reliably be defined, in general concepts by consensus or "natural law," and in detail by positive law. So *what* the rules are is not up for discussion here.

On what philosophical grounds we should accept *particular* rules (appeal to custom, the legislator's authority, the will of God revealed, personal happiness, social contract, social hygiene . . .) is likewise not undertaken here.

---

[1] Clarification of some of the following formulations and of their logical differences has been aided by comments of Notre Dame colleagues, especially Dr. Captain King Pfeiffer (USN. ret.) and Professor Robert Rodes.

1. Chivalry: It is part of the vocational dignity of the knight that he would rather lose a combat or even his life than not fight according to the rules. The rule is self-enforcing. It is part of the dignity of his elite vocation as knight. This is more like sportsmanship or etiquette than it is like morality or law. Is this what "honor" means in American military education? How distinctive is the strand of chivalry in the development of concepts of restraint?

2. Cultural anthropology: "Let the gods decide." War is a forensic combat, fought according to ritual game rules, an "ordeal" that leaves the judgment to the gods or to God. Until the war is over, it cannot be held that the enemies' cause is wrong. Breaking the rules of the game means:
   a. We cannot be honestly invoking divine judgment;
   b. We may prevent the gods from using the combat to reveal their verdict.

3. Reverent monotheism: "The Almighty has his own purposes." This stance agrees with #2 above in its reverence for God's sovereignty over the course of events, which calls us to fight by the rules, but it posits in addition:
   a. The Almighty is unique, sovereign, with inscrutable designs;
   b. God's purposes may include our suffering, as retribution for past injustice.

4. Divine command: This is also a form of #3 above, but instead of yielding to God's control of history, we keep the rules out of reverence for God's revealed imperative to respect the life and dignity of our neighbor, whom the rules protect. It would be wrong to "ground" the authority of the divine command anywhere else than in itself. This is the primary way the Catholic tradition teaches about lying and adultery.

5. Reciprocal utility: If both parties respect the same contracted restraints, the total damage will be reduced, and war can still have the limited function of readjusting power relations among nations. If we keep the rules, our enemy is more likely to do so too, and that will be better for all parties concerned. Soldiers see one another as colleagues, and both sides have a stake in respect for the rules. If soldiers know they will be given quarter, they are more likely to surrender when beaten, hoping to live to fight again, thus saving lives and shortening the war. This is a special subcase of the general

theory of moral discourse called *rule-utility*. We obey the rules because respecting a pattern of most people keeping most of the rules most of the time is best for us all, even though for the individual, or in the case of specific decisions, there will be times when rigorous respect for all the rules is not the most advantageous choice for me.

6. The credibility of the social contract. An intensified form of reason applies in a society where rules are adopted by democratic due process and respected not only because of the threat of police punishment but as a matter of conscience and mutual respect. We keep the rules because we share a stake in the credibility of the order as a whole. If we make exceptions in our favor, we cannot object if others do.

7. Reciprocal threats and fear of reprisal: If we break the rules, the enemy can claim the right to do the same. It is therefore in the interest of both parties to respect the rules.

8. Covenant: We should respect the restraints laid down in international agreements because our nation is a signatory to them. *Pacta sunt servanda*, "Agreements are to keep." Once a solemn promise has been made, no further reasons are needed for it to be binding; its bindingness is specifically *not* dependent on proving what we gain by obeying. The Constitution of the U.S.A. (Art. VI) makes treaties "the supreme law of the land."

9. Sworn fidelity: We should respect the rules laid down in the code of the military conduct of our country, because they are the law which we have sworn to uphold. An oath makes an obligation morally binding, as a simple affirmation or signature would not.

10. Obligations of nobility: Even if the enemy breaks the rules, we will not; honor is what war is about. If we were to descend to the enemy's level, we would have lost the war morally, even if our side might "win" the contest of brute force. That the enemy did something bad is not a reason that we should do it. We would prefer to lose, having fought honorably, rather than to win through cheating or brutality. Such a loss due to integrity would be a moral victory. This view is somewhat like #1 above (chivalry), but it applies to the moral dignity of the nation as a whole, or to the armed forces as a whole, not only to elite officers ("knights").

11. Liability: If we commit a war crime and are caught, we may be tried and punished by our victorious enemies (Nuremberg) or even by our own authorities (My Lai).

12. Ritual impurity (exemplified by medieval canon law): Shedding blood renders Christians unacceptable before God, and disqualifies them from receiving the sacraments. That impurity must be purged or expiated by the passage of time and by penitential deeds, such as pilgrimages. Even bloodshed that was legally and morally legitimate, as in a justified war, calls for purgation; unjustified bloodshed calls for more. This consideration is very weighty in explaining the *general* abhorrence of bloodshed in medieval Christian thought and in explaining priestly immunity. It, however, does not link *directly* to a distinct reason for keeping the *in bello* rules, since:
    a. A priest was not supposed to fight even in a justified war;
    b. A soldier who killed even in a just war needed absolution.

Thus far, although each "reason" given for keeping rules leaves the concrete content of the rules to be specified, they all connect specifically with war as an institution. The following considerations also belong in the discussion, but they are broader. They have to do with *any* context in which one "does what is right" at some cost. *In bello* compliance with the rules of the just-war tradition is obviously one of the very important places where this readiness to do the right at some cost is tested, but in terms of philosophical method the same reasons would have to apply no less to truth-telling, promise-keeping, sexual fidelity, non-stealing, and so on.

13. Pure obligation: We do the right only because it is right. To do the right for any other reason than its pure rightness would downgrade the sense of natural moral obligation.

14. Laws of nature: According to Grotius, the laws of nature are not "silent" even when the peaceable order of nature and the domestic positive laws which presuppose that order are destroyed.

15. Loving intention: A loving (subjective) intention toward all fellow humans demands that we fight only to protect the truly innocent against the truly guilty, because we love everyone, even the enemy, and are willing to sacrifice ourselves. The "rules" are a welcome aid in holding ourselves to that intention.

16. There is always something more important than winning. That "something" may be the same as the nobility of #10 above, the moral absolute of #4 or #13, or the knightly honor of #1. It may also be some other personal or national moral value. In the case of the United States, it may be the nation's moral and legal commitment to "the Rule of Law."

   a. All these variants have in common that they reject ordinary "realist" arguments to the effect that we have to do what we have to do, that there is no substitute for victory.

   b. This dictum may be interpreted consequentially as saying that other values (honor, the character of being one who keeps his word, the rule of law) are greater than victory.
   Or,

   c. It may be an anti-consequentialist argument, parallel to #13-15 above.

17. Causal unity of ends and means: Evil means cannot serve a good end, even though in specific extreme cases it may look as if they might. This was the argument of Gandhi against all violence. It is the argument of many against lying. It may also be the argument of an honorable soldier against *in bello* just-war infractions.

18. Moral unity of rhetoric and method: We cannot deny in action what we say we are for in principle. As a matter of fact, of course, we *can*, but to do so decreases our credibility to ourselves and others.

Questions to Be Answered
against the Background of the Above List

   1. Historically: Are there reasons in the history of Western thought other than the above that have been important in restraining war?

   2. Historically: Which of the above considerations would be closer to the understanding of Augustine? of Vitoria? of Lieber?

   3. Psychologically: If you were an officer in a critical command situation, where the immediate necessity of the situation seemed to demand that you risk the security or the lives of persons under your command or act *against* the law of war, which, if any, of the above considerations would move you to respect the rules despite the cost?

   4. Sociologically: Which, if any, of the above modes of moral response are/is most likely to be convincing in a setting of cultural plural-

ism and secularism? Which, if any, would move "the American people" to reject an unjust war?

5. Philosophically: Can the above arguments be classified in standard methodological terms as rooted in duty, in utility, in virtue, in covenant, and so on?

6. Philosophically: There is a standard paradox involved in asking why we would keep rules "at cost to ourselves." Consequential reasoning calculates costs and benefits. Other forms of moral reasoning (#1, 3-5, 8-10, 13-15 and 16b above), while recognizing that right action is costly, do not base their rightness on such a cost calculation. The predictable evil is never sure. It is therefore never necessary to argue that to rule out a morally unacceptable alternative will be sure to have specified evil consequences. Therefore, "what would we rather lose than do?" is not a proper (or not a logically possible) question.

The Laws of War in Modern Treaties

This listing is provided to give the reader a sense of the long diplomatic history through which the definition of the laws of war in the form of treaties was developed. The list could be much fuller, and the process of negotiation, now under the auspices of the United Nations, continues to expand the series.[1]

1856　Paris Declaration: Maritime law—no privateering, status of neutral goods, rules for blockades; fourteen signers

1864　Geneva: Red Cross convention, treatment of the wounded

1868　St. Petersburg Declaration: no explosive projectiles under 400 grams; seventeen signers

1874　Brussels Declaration: twenty-seven signers (never ratified)
- administration of occupied populations;
- militia forces treated as soldiers;
- forbidden weapons;
- no attacking unfortified towns;
- whom to treat as spies;
- humane treatment of prisoners;
- no confiscating private property, no pillage;

---

[1] Sources for the following list are: Leon Friedman, ed., *The Law of War: A Documentary History* (New York: Random House, 1972); and Adam Roberts, ed., *Documents on the Laws of War* (Oxford: Clarendon, 1982).

- armistices;
- neutrals.

1899 The Hague
I. Peaceful settlements; international court
II. Laws of land war (carried over from Brussels 1874 above)
III. Geneva convention (1864) applied to maritime warfare; hospital ships, wounded prisoners;
IV.1 No projectiles launched from balloons
IV.2 No expanding bullets
IV.3 No projectiles carrying gases

1906 Geneva Red Cross Declaration: care of wounded and prisoners; medical material and personnel exempt from capture; use and abuse of the Red Cross emblem

1907 The Hague
I. Pacific settlement of disputes: mediation, arbitration
II. Limiting use of war to collect debts due to citizens of one nation
III. Opening of hostilities; no hostilities without prior warning, ultimatum, or declaration
IV. Laws and customs of land war; belligerent status, prisoners, forbidden weapons, truces, occupied territories. For example, Article XXIII lists as prohibited:
- to use poison or poisoned weapons;
- to kill or wound treacherously;
- to kill or wound a surrendered enemy;
- to declare that no quarter will be given;
- to use arms calculated to cause unnecessary suffering;
- to use improperly a flag of truce, enemy flag, or Red Cross;
- to cause unnecessary destruction or seizure of enemy property;
- to suspend the rights of enemy nationals;
- to compel enemy nationals to take part in hostilities against their own country.
V. Neutral powers and persons
VI. Enemy merchant ships at outbreak of hostilities; not confiscated
VII. Conversion of merchant ships into warships

VIII. Submarine mines: forbidden unless anchored; shippers must be told where they are; must deactivate if it comes loose from anchors; torpedoes must deactivate after missing target; must be removed after war ends

IX. Naval bombardment: no bombardment of undefended towns, ports, unless the authorities refuse to provide needed supplies

X. Applying Geneva convention (1906) to maritime warfare

XI. Restricting rights of capture: postal ships, fishing, scientific, philanthropic vessels exempted; personnel of captured enemy ships who are neutral nationals exempted

XII. Prize court: status of the cargo of neutral ships; neutral-owned cargo of enemy ships; enemy ships taken in neutral waters

XIII. Neutral powers in naval wars: neutral may neither support either belligerent nor be forced to

XIV. No explosives or projectiles from balloons

1909 London Naval Conference: blockades; what may and may not be contraband; defining neutrality

1919 Versailles: creation of the League of Nations

1922-23 The Hague: rules of air warfare; limits of legitimate bombardment; compensation for damages beyond legitimate targets

1922 Washington: submarines and noxious gases; merchant vessel not to be attacked unless first stopped and searched—which means, in effect, no use of submarines in war (this item was to become the classic example of a "dead letter"); no use of poison gases

1925 Geneva: extend to bacteriological weapons the prohibitions of gas

1928 Havana: inter-American convention on maritime neutrality

1928 Paris (Kellogg-Briand): renounce war as instrument of policy

1929 Geneva Red Cross convention (updating 1906)

1929   Geneva: prisoners of war

1945   August 8 Four Power Agreement: chartering International Military Tribunal for the prosecution and punishment of war crimes in the European Theater ("Nuremberg")

1946   January Declaration by General MacArthur constituting International Military Tribunal for the Far East

1948   United Nations: prohibition of genocide

1949   Geneva: wounded on land (updating 1929)

1949   Geneva II: wounded at sea

1949   Geneva III: prisoners

1949   Geneva IV: protection of civilians

1954   The Hague: Protection of cultural property

1961   Geneva: Nuclear weapons direct violation of the charter of the United Nations

1968   United Nations: on human rights; no direct attack on civilian populations

1969   United Nations: report of Secretary General on better application of existing conventions

1970   United Nations: report on human rights in armed conflicts:
    IX.   When guerrillas should be treated as privileged combatants;
    X.   Protection of civilian populations in liberation struggles

1970   United Nations Resolution: protection of civilians

1971   United Nations: two protocols on care of the sick and wounded (updating 1949)

1971   Zagreb: conflicts where United Nations forces are involved

1972 Washington/London/Moscow: prohibition of bacteriological and toxic weapons

1977 United Nations: no military use of environmental modification

1981 United Nations: excessive use of conventional weapons

Criteria of the Just-War Tradition

Everyone agrees that the just-war tradition consists of a set of criteria to be used to test whether a war (or a particular activity within a war) is justified. The criteria are commonsensical. Yet as we have already observed, there is not a single, standard, normative list.[1] We need, therefore, to make our own listing of the main concerns of the tradition.[2]

The criteria here gathered in a logical order are telescoped chronologically over the centuries. For many items in the list sources are cited. The intent of the citation is not proof but illustration, in order to provide the reader with a sense of the texture of the centuries-long conversation and also of the contextual and dated quality of many of the statements. Some were at home in medieval times and are considered inappropriate now. Nonetheless, their place in history may teach us something about the logic of the tradition. Occasionally in this list, therefore, a provision most clearly at home in medieval times and not taken seriously now is labeled (MA). Other statements have been elaborated only recently. No attempt is here made to clarify the logically important internal questions which must arise in the application of these criteria, such as:

- how the varied criteria interlock,
- whether they ever contradict one another,

---

[1] There are many sources for lists of *jus ad bellum* criteria. These include the *Modern Catholic Encyclopedia* (1994), which lists seven, including comparative justice as a criterion. See also James Turner Johnson's many books on the subject, including *Can Modern War Be Just?* (1984), 3.

[2] Aid in clarifying some of these formulations was generously given by Professor R. Rodes, who is, however, not responsible for the overall outline.

• whether any have priority over others, or
• how completely they must be met.

The reader is undoubtedly aware from the rest of the book that all of these questions are also crucial as to whether the system can work to give shape to firm decisions.

I.   War may be waged only by a *legitimate authority*.

A.   Criteria for a legitimate ruler:
1.   dynastic descent from a previous ruler;
2.   election according to custom or constitution;
3.   legitimacy may be forfeited by being a bad ruler or "tyrant"; thus "justice" or "good government" or de facto ability to govern may be indirectly a criterion: "The kingdom is forfeited if a king sets out with a truly hostile intent to destroy a whole people" (Grotius, *On the Law of War and Peace*, I.IV.11);
4.   religious heresy may be held to disqualify a ruler; thus religious orthodoxy may become a part of legitimacy (this arises c. 1600, see I/B/4/d below).

B.   This criterion of legitimacy excludes:
1.   war by private citizens (except in emergency defense) (see Thomas, ST II-II, Q. 40, art. 1);
2.   war by bandits or privateers;
3.   war between political units not on the same level;
4.   war against one's own sovereign (see Grotius, *On the Law of War and Peace*, I.IV.7, 15). For much of the history of the just-war tradition rebellion is not admitted. Later it comes to be admitted under conditions:
   a.   that an evil ruler has forfeited the right to rule (see I/A/3; cf. Grotius, *On the Law of War and Peace*, I.IV.8);
   b.   that "lesser magistrates" with a clearly just cause act to resist the ruler (e.g., Magna Carta) or to depose the tyrant;
   c.   (hypothetically) that the entire people rises up "as one";
   d.   that the ruler becomes illegitimate by persecuting true religion.[3]

---

[3] After 1573 the Huguenots (French Protestants) said this about Catholic kings. At the same time the Jesuits said it about the Queen of England. It would appear that before the Reformation, a ruler's supporting heresy would have been grounds for ecclesiastical condemnation, including excommunication, but not for revolution.

C. Only a soldier under oath and under the control of the sovereign may fight.

  1. Clergy, religious, and penitents are excluded or dispensed: "But the thought of warlike matters seems to be foreign to the duty of our office, for we have our thoughts fixed more on the duty of the soul than on that of the body; nor is it our business to look to arms, but rather to the affairs of peace" (Ambrose, *On the Duties of the Clergy*, I.35).

    a. military orders (Knights Templar, Knights of Malta) in a crusade are exceptions, with a special episcopal mandate, to the exclusion of clergy;

    b. since the inception of conscription, the churches have tended to consider clergy exemption as a right that Western governments theoretically ought to grant, but most churches have not usually made it an issue. Clergy have generally not refused to serve if drafted, although in canon law they should have that right. A man who has killed in even a just war is disqualified from becoming a priest (MA).

  2. A mercenary may only hire on to fight for a cause he knows is just (MA).[4]

D. Sometimes the question of authority to wage war is confused with that of authority to decide when a war is just.

  1. Since the criteria of the just war are objective, and since the facts they measure are verifiable, any moralist, lawyer, journalist, or counsellor to a king can make the judgment on a particular war or weapon, though there is room for honest difference on some details. Especially a bishop would have that authority. This can be tested in international tribunals or by third-party mediation or arbitration: "Senators and petty rulers and in general all who are admitted on summons or voluntarily to the public council or the prince's council ought, and are bound, to examine into the cause of an unjust war. . . . Again, a king is not by himself capable of examining into the causes of a war and the possibility of a mistake on his part is not unlikely and such a mistake would bring great evil and ruin to multitudes. Therefore, war ought not to be made on the

---

[4] Geneva 1977 condemns mercenaries. During the first millennium of the just-war tradition, however, it was not assumed that soldiers needed to be citizens of the nation they fought for.

sole judgment of the king, nor, indeed, on the judgment of a few, but on that of many, and they wise and upright men" (Vitoria, *On the Law of War*, para. 24).

In modern democratic thought, citizens can and should test a decision made by their government.

2. The facts on the basis of which a decision is made may however not always be publicly accessible or seen in the same light by all concerned. This makes it possible for both sides (or the public, the subjects on both sides of a conflict) to think they are in the right.[5]

3. A crusade in the canonical sense, which entitles the soldiers to indulgences, can be declared only by an episcopal council, pope, or prophet (MA).

II. A war may be fought only for a *just cause*.

A. The offense must be:

1. actual, not only possible;
2. intentional, not inadvertent or unintended or an honest error;
3. of substantial importance;
   a. it is wrong to go to war for a trifle: "It is not lawful for slight wrongs to pursue the authors of the wrongs of war" (Vitoria, *On the Law of War*, para. 14);
   b. the selfish interests of the princely house do not suffice; the whole community's interests and rights must be at stake: "Neither the personal glory of the prince nor any other advantage to him is a just cause of war" (ibid., para. 12).
4. objective, verifiable, as to fact;
5. unilateral, not provoked. If there is doubt as to the provocation, the recourse is to arbitrate. However, a just cause might arise if in a process of escalation the side responsible for a provocation sought to make amends, and the other party attacked anyway.

---

[5] At least since Emmerich de Vattell's *The Law of Nations; or Principles of the Law of Nature: Applied to the Conduct and Affairs of Nations and Sovereigns* (1740) this phenomenon is taken seriously. Since each side may believe its cause is just, and nothing but the war itself can adjudicate that difference, respect for just means becomes relatively more important. This is called *simultaneous ostensible justice*.

B. The offense may be:
1. an aggression demanding defense or a threat demanding deterrence;
2. an injustice demanding reparation, such as:
    a. seizure of property;
    b. denial of free passage on land or sea;
    c. breach of treaty obligations;
    d. insult to the honor of nation or sovereign (MA) (see Vitoria, *On the Law of War.* para. 19);
    e. failure of a government to punish or make reparation for its subjects' crimes, or to make them pay their debts;
    f. interference with the passage of pilgrims, with the freedom of missionaries, or with the worship of a subject Christian population (MA) (see Thomas, ST II-II, Q. 10, art. 8).

C. The offense may be committed against a third nation:
1. against one's ally: "Next to subjects, and indeed on an equal footing with them in this respect, that they ought to be defended, are allies, in whose treaty of alliance this obligation is embraced" (Grotius, *On the Law of War and Peace*, II.XXV.4). This was the U.S. claim in Vietnam and in Kuwait.
2. against some innocent subjects on whose behalf a third party intervenes "on humanitarian grounds." This was recently done by India in Bangladesh and by Tanzania in Uganda, considered by the United Nations for Somalia and by the European Union for Bosnia.

D. The *cause* may be moral guilt demanding punishment:
1. heresy, blasphemy, other offenses against God's honor (MA);
2. violations of the laws of nature and the rights of peoples. In colonial times it was held, for example, that European intervention in South America, Africa, and Asia was justified by the practices of cannibalism, human sacrifice, or sexual immorality by natives, or by their natural inferiority, or by their inability by themselves to govern themselves or build a civilization;
3. violations of the laws of nations needing to be punished in the interest of world order.

III. A war may be fought only with a *right intention*.
Intention in the objective sense *(finis operis)* is the goal or end of the entire military/political enterprise, which must be justified in terms of the global common good.

A. The only valid objective intention is the restoration of peace; that is, the creation of a total world state of affairs better than what would obtain without the intervention: "Peace should be the object of your desire; war should be waged only as a necessity, and waged only that God may by it deliver men from the necessity and preserve them in peace. For peace is not sought in order to the kindling of war, but war is waged in order that peace may be obtained" (Augustine, "Letter to Boniface," para. 16).
     This universal commonweal includes the enemy's real best interests.[6] It may contradict the notion of punishment (II/D).

B. National honor, territorial or commercial aggrandizement, and the weakening or destruction of enemy regimes are not in themselves valid ends, although they may be served by activities justified on other grounds.

C. This is one reason unconditional surrender is an inappropriate demand. The right intention should always be present in the form of the publicly stated terms of peace always offered to the enemy.

IV. A war may be fought only with *right intention*.
Intention in the subjective sense *(finis operantis)* is motivation, or attitude.

A. Inadmissible intentions are:
    1. hatred, vengefulness, enmity;
    2. cruelty, love of violence;
    3. desire for power or fame;
    4. material gain (booty, slaves, or territory) (Thomas, ST II-II, Q. 40, art. I).
    The cause may be justified, but participation may still be sinful if the intention is wrong in one of these ways.

---

[6] John A. Ryan and Francis Boland, *Catholic Principles of Politics* (New York: The Macmillan Co., 1947), 260.

B. Valid components of subjective intention:
   1. love for the victims of the aggression: "Now it is in the love of innocent men that both capital punishment and just wars have their origin" (Grotius, *On the Law of War and Peace*, I.II.8 and 10);
   2. trust in God;
   3. willingness to face risk or sacrifice;
   4. love for the enemy, desire to restore him to righteousness (see Augustine, "Letter to Marcellinus," chap. II, para. 14);
   5. humility and regret at the needfulness of the evil of war: "Wars and conquests may rejoice unprincipled men, but are a sad necessity in the eyes of men of principle" (Augustine, *City of God*, IV.15). Roland Bainton characterizes Augustine as being "mournful" in yielding to war's necessity.[7]

C. Showing mercy after winning is frequently listed as a criterion. It cannot be measured, except as a stated intention, before the war. If sincerely intended, it will make a difference in the choice of means.
   1. Do not use means which will interfere with the reestablishment of peace after the war: "Military necessity does not include any act of hostility which makes the return to peace unnecessarily difficult."[8]
   2. When the war is over it will not be marked by triumphal self-congratulation, but by somber regret for the victims.[9]

D. *The Challenge of Peace* (1983) added to the classical list a new term—*comparative justice*. This term seems at first to denote a call to modesty about the imperfections of one's own society, and thereby to make it more difficult to meet the criteria of cause or authority.
   1. In actual usage (as *The Challenge of Peace* was concerned primarily with the USSR as adversary), the notion that "nobody's

---

[7] Bainton, *Christian Attitudes toward War and Peace*, 98.

[8] Francis Lieber, "General Orders No. 100: Instructions for the Government of Armies of the United States in the Field" (approved by President Lincoln in 1863), art. XVI.

[9] Schuck, "When the Shooting Stops: Missing Elements in Just War Theory," 982ff.

perfect" tends to work in the opposite direction. It tends to undercut concrete discrimination, as long as our cause is (in our minds) "relatively" better than the enemy's. The worse the enemy, the less hard we need to be on ourselves. This view was accentuated by certain critics who held that if the evils of Soviet imperialism provide the "just cause," concern for legitimate means could be set aside.

2. The intent of the author who added this term (Bryan Hehir) was something else again, namely, to recognize the fact that both sides may *think* they have the just cause,[10] and the obligation to respect the entire set of just-war criteria should not depend on all the wrong being on one side (see V/F below).

3. No ethicist has followed the bishops in adding this criterion to the classical list. (The 1994 *Catholic Encyclopedia* added it without taking account of its novelty.) It is in fact not a criterion (a criterion is something to measure by) but rather one additional consideration (or two) to keep in mind when thinking about just cause.

The above categories (I-IV) are generally grouped under the heading *jus ad bellum*; that is, the law having to do with going to war or "the right to fight." Until these criteria have been met, there is no need to discuss proper means.

V. Due Process: A war is illegitimate unless the criteria apply with procedural integrity.

The phrases "due process" and "procedural integrity" are modern. They do not appear in the standard documents. They do, however, enable a helpful clarification. The items grouped here appear on all the standard lists as qualifying phrases, whether under cause, intention, authority or means. Because of their procedural quality, and because they apply both *ad bellum* and *in bello*, it is fitting that we should group them here under a separate heading.

A. War must be a last resort, only after everything else has been tried. Refusal of other resources for redress invalidates an otherwise just complaint.[11] Such other resources are:

---

[10] See above, note 5 at I/D/2 and in chapter 7, the section entitled "*The Challenge of Peace* as Moral Guidance," pages 88ff. above.

[11] Ryan and Boland, *Catholic Principles of Politics*, 150, 256-57.

1. negotiation, mediation, arbitration: in the Middle Ages episcopal mediation or arbitration could be effective (cf. recent mediation by the pope between Argentina and Chile);
2. recourse to international tribunals and good offices;
3. "cooling off" time, time for the enemy to back down;
4. the formality of a declaration of war, preceded by a warning, followed by time to sue for peace (see Cicero, *De Officiis*, I.11).[12]
5. The war goals must be stated:
   a. as an act of accountability to the world community (see Grotius, *On the Law of War and Peace*, II.XXVI.4, 7);
   b. so that the enemy may at any time sue for peace on those terms.

B. The enemy must always be able to sue for peace:
   1. the war goal may not be unconditional surrender;
   2. pursuing hostilities beyond reasonable redress makes a previously valid cause unjust;
   3. pursuing hostilities when the enemy has offered to negotiate makes the cause unjust;
   4. this is the other side of the notion of last resort.

C. There must be respect for international law, customs, treaties, and international agencies.

D. The entire war must promise to be proportionately prudent, that is, to cause less harm than the harm it seeks to prevent: "To have recourse to violent warfare it is not enough to have to defend overall against any kind of injustice. If the injury caused by warfare exceeds the injury suffered by tolerating the injustice done, one may be obliged to suffer that particular injustice."[13] (For classic statements, see Vitoria, *On the Law of War*, para. 33; and Grotius, *On the Law of War and Peace*, II.XXIV.9).

E. The war must be winnable, otherwise one suffers both evils (the evil to be prevented and the evil of war).

---

[12] Ibid., 164, 262.

[13] Pope Pius XII, Address to the XVIth Congress of the International Bureau of Documentation on Military Medicine (October 19, 1953), *Dicorsi e Radiomessaggi* XV, 422.

    1. This follows obviously from proportionality and is a safeguard against crusading enthusiasms.

    2. However, some versions of the just-war tradition make an exception for heroic self-defense, even if hopeless.

F. Objectively a war can be just only on one side. Subjectively, however, both parties may believe in good faith that they are in the right.

    1. This is the reason for third-party involvement (V/A).

    2. This is why subjects or citizens or soldiers should not accept their ruler's word unquestioningly.

    3. In individual battles citizens even on the erring side have a right to defend themselves. Thus the fact that they do so cannot be considered a war crime.

    4. This is why enemy combatants who fight fairly (*in bello*) deserve respectful and legal treatment, however wrong we think their cause.

A war may be fought only by the use of legitimate means, *jus in bello*, "fighting right." This is the second major traditional category.

VI. Means must be indispensable, the only way, "necessary."

A. Unnecessary combat is to be avoided even in a just cause.

B. During combat no unnecessary death or wanton destruction may be inflicted (see Cicero, *De Officiis*, I.11 I.24).

C. What commanders consider necessary has different meanings:

    1. Legal texts name necessity as a requisite *within* what the rest of the rules allow.[14]

    2. Much argument in popular and political settings, however, appeals to necessity as grounds for *breaking* the rules.[15] Then necessity is not a criterion but an argument for indulgence.

VII. Means must be proportional.

A. The damage must not be greater than the damage prevented or the offense being avenged.

---

[14]Lieber, "U.S. Army Field Manual," art. XIV.
[15]See Walzer, *Just and Unjust Wars*, 2d ed., 251ff., 323ff.

B. The damage or punishment inflicted must not be disproportionate to the guilt of the offender (this cannot apply to particular battles).

C. Proportion must be tested on every level—a given weapon, a tactic, a strategy, a given battle. A measure that appears disproportionate on one level may appear proportionate on a higher one; for example, the disproportionate cost of one battle may be held to be outweighed if it wins the war. The modest cost of a battle, on the other hand, may be wrong if the war is already lost.

VIII. The means used must respect the immunity of the innocent.
"The deliberate slaughter of the innocent is never lawful in itself. . . . Wrong is not done by an innocent person. Therefore war may not be employed against him. . . . Hence it follows that even in war with the Turks it is not allowable to kill children. This is clear, because they are innocent. Aye, and the same holds with regard to the women of unbelievers" (Vitoria, *On the Law of War*, paras. 35f).

A. *Innocent* means those who are no threat:
    1. women, children, the aged, infirm;
    2. clergy, religious, foreigners;
    3. unarmed persons going about their ordinary vocations;
    4. even soldiers on leave or who have become prisoners.

B. *Innocent* does not mean that persons are not patriotic, do not morally support the war effort, or do not participate in the wartime economy, but only that they are no threat, are not combatant: "A quite obstinate devotion to one's own party, provided only that the cause is not altogether dishonorable, does not deserve punishment. . . . Or, if such devotion is punished in any way, the penalty should not be carried so far as death, for no just judge would so decide" (Grotius, *On the Law of War and Peace*, III.XI.16). The clarity of this criterion has recently been compromised, though not logically set aside, by the notion of a quasi-combatant work force.

C. Obviously the innocent include neutral third parties.

D. Special offenses against the innocent are:
    1. reprisals and the taking or killing of hostages;
    2. terrorism.

E. But noncombatants may come into jeopardy indirectly
    1. by staying in a besieged city;
    2. by being close to a military target.

F. Even combatants may be killed only when they are a threat:
    1. a surrendered soldier may not be killed;
    2. a soldier returned to civilian life may not be killed;
    3. after the war, those guilty of war crimes may be punished only
        by due process:
        a. as vengeance/correction (MA);
        b. as deterrence/prevention;
        c. as part of the rule of law needing no other justification;
        d. but there should be mercy if possible.

G. Slaves may be taken (MA), but not if the defeated soldiers or the
    subjugated population is Christian.

IX. The means used must be discriminating, that is, subjected to measured control.

This is prerequisite if proportionality (VII) and noncombatant immunity (VIII) are to be respected. If any weapon, any strategy, any military unit becomes uncontrollable, then that abandonment of discrimination infringes in principle upon the discipline of necessary and legitimate means, *even if* the illicit actions have not yet been taken. If any government or command center *says* it intends to strike indiscriminately, that is already immoral as intention even though it has not been carried out.[16]

X. The means used must respect the dignity of humankind as rational and social.

A. No slander.

B. No unnatural cruelty (mutilation, torture).

C. Keeping faith with the enemy (truces, safe conducts, no treason, perfidy, perjury).

---

[16] This logic becomes especially important in the nuclear case, but it would also apply to "scorched earth," "ethnic cleansing," and other intrinsically indiscriminate policies.

D. Lying is always wrong (although one may use ambush and subterfuge or permit the enemy to gather false impressions) (see Thomas, ST II-II, Q. 40, art. 3).[17]

E. There is to be no pillage and no destruction of property unless the enemy might use it. Even when sacking a city can be justified to deprive the enemy of its resources, the women should not be raped, or the temples plundered, or the fruit trees cut.

F. Do not poison wells or rivers.

G. Do not fight on holy days (MA) or during times of proclaimed truce.

H. Do not profane churches or cemeteries; respect sanctuary (MA).

I. Give quarter; that is, do not kill even in combat an enemy who surrenders.

XI. Means used must not be forbidden by positive law or treaties (V/C above).

In medieval times such prohibitions were part of canon law, but since all the rulers of Europe claimed to be Christian and Catholic, they were valid civil law as well. They included the Third Lateran Council (1139) prohibition against the crossbow and the Fourth Lateran Council (1215) prohibition against the catapult.

A. For example, the following precisely defined prohibitions figure in articles XXII and XXIII of Convention IV of The Hague (1907)[18]:

1. to employ poison or poisoned weapons;
2. to kill or wound treacherously individuals belonging to the hostile nation or army;

---

[17] Aquinas's argument in this article is not that a particular kind of lying is not wrong, but that a particular kind of subterfuge is not deception or lying. All lying remains wrong, as it did for Augustine. The total prohibition on lying in war is reiterated in all seriousness by Charles Macksey in the 1912/13 *Catholic Encyclopedia* (vol. 15, 549).

[18] Article XXII of the Regulations Annexed to The Hague Convention of 1907 states that "the right of belligerents to adopt means of injuring the enemy is not unlimited."

3. to kill or wound an enemy who, having laid down his arms, or having no longer means of defense, has surrendered;
4. to declare that no quarter will be given;
5. to employ arms, projectiles, or material calculated to cause unnecessary suffering;
6. to make improper use of a flag of truce, of the national flag, or of the military insignia and uniform of the enemy, as well as the distinctive badges of the Geneva Convention (e.g., Red Cross);
7. to destroy or seize the enemy's property, unless such destruction or seizure be imperatively demanded by the necessities of war;
8. to declare abolished, suspended, or inadmissible in a court of law the rights and actions of the nationals of the hostile party.

B. A belligerent is forbidden to compel the nationals of the hostile party to take part in the operations of war directed against their own country, even if they were in the belligerent's service before the commencement of the war.

C. Respect for the Peace of God or the Truce of God when declared by the competent episcopal authority (MA).

D. Respect for cease-fire agreements.

E. Occupied populations should be governed justly. Soldiers who surrender must not be killed. Spies and terrorists, however, forfeit these rights.

F. For many of these matters there are extensive international agreements that define and defend the pertinent rights and obligations (e.g., XI/A above). The degree of bindingness of specific treaty rules varies.
1. depending on whether one nation has signed the convention;
2. depending on whether the other party has signed; the declarations of Paris (1856) and St. Petersburg (1868) specify that they are not binding when fighting a non-signatory;
3. depending on whether the other party has belligerent status.

Yet morally, the bindingness of the rights at stake does not depend on whether texts were signed by all parties. The particular formulations were defined in particular texts, but the rules based in moral and customary law apply to all.

Questions Involved in Evaluating and/or Espousing and/or Implementing the Above System

- Is each criterion defined so concretely that its application would be clear if you (as citizen, as military commander, as field combatant, moral consultant, chaplain, journalist) were responsible for making rulings on particular cases?

- Is each criterion listed above logically convincing to you? If you were at war would you agree that your belligerency should respect these restraints? Would you grant your enemy's right to attack you under these conditions?

- If there is any criterion listed above by which you would not want to be bound, would you then agree that your adversary need not respect it either?

- Would it be possible to implement these criteria by teaching them to soldiers?
  — If you are an ROTC student, do you already know them or expect to be responsible to learn them?
  — If you are a simple citizen, do you want the military commanders and combatants who prepare for and engage in combat in your name to know and respect them? Is that realistic?

- Could one win a war while respecting all of these rules?

Bibliography

As this book is intended as a guide to further study, the sources indicated here go well beyond what is needed to support the material covered in the text. Beyond the items listed here under three headings, abundant further bibliographical guidance is given in the works by Roland Bainton, Jonathan Barnes, and especially James Turner Johnson.

Primary Bibliography on the Just-War Tradition

Bainton, Roland. *Christian Attitudes toward War and Peace*. New York: Abingdon Press, 1960.

Barnes, Jonathan. "The Just War." In Norman Kreutzmann, Anthony Kenny, and Jan Pinborg, eds., *The Cambridge History of Later Medieval Philosophy: From the Rediscovery of Aristotle to the Disintegration of Scholasticism 1100-1600*. New York: Cambridge University Press, 1982.

Cahill, Lisa Sowle. *Love Your Enemies: Discipleship, Pacifism, and Just War Theory*. Minneapolis: Fortress Press, 1994.

Childress, James. *Moral Responsibility in Conflicts: Essays on Nonviolence, War, and Conscience*. Baton Rouge: Louisiana State University Press, 1982.

Elshtain, Jean Bethke, ed. *Just-War Theory*. New York: New York University Press, 1992.

_____ . *Women and War*. 2d ed. Chicago: University of Chicago Press, 1995.

Friedman, Leon, comp. *The Law of War, A Documentary History*. New York: Random House, 1972.

International Union of Social Studies. *A Code of International Ethics*. Paris: Editions Spes, 1937; Oxford: Catholic Social Guild, 1937; Westminster, Md.: Newman Press, 1953.

Johnson, James Turner. *Can Modern War Be Just?* New Haven: Yale University Press, 1985.

163

_____ . *Ideology, Reason and the Limitation of War: Religious and Secular Concepts 1200-1740.* Princeton, N.J.: Princeton University Press, 1975.

_____ . *The Just War and Jihad: Historical and Theoretical Perspectives on War and Peace in Western and Islamic Traditions.* New York: Greenwood Press, 1991.

_____ . *The Just War Tradition and the Restraint of War.* Princeton, N.J.: Princeton University Press, 1981.

_____ . *The Quest for Peace: Three Moral Traditions in Western Cultural History.* Princeton, N.J.: Princeton University Press, 1987.

_____ , with George Weigel. *The Just War and the Gulf War.* Washington, D.C.: Ethics and Public Policy Center, 1991.

McNeal, Patricia. *Harder than War.* New Brunswick: Rutgers University Press, 1992.

Miller, Richard B. *Interpretations of Conflict: Ethics, Pacifism, and the Just War Tradition.* Chicago: University of Chicago Press, 1991.

_____ , ed. *War in the Twentieth Century: Sources in Theological Ethics.* Louisville, Ky.: Westminster/John Knox Press, 1992.

National Council of Catholic Bishops (NCCB). *The Harvest of Justice is Sown in Peace.* Washington, D.C.: USCC, 1994. Also available in *Origins* 23/26 (December 9, 1993), 450-64.

O'Brien, William V. *The Conduct of Just and Limited War.* New York: Praeger Press, 1981.

Ramsey, Paul. *The Just War: Force and Political Responsibility.* New York: Scribners Press, 1968.

_____ . *War and Christian Conscience: How Shall Modern War Be Conducted Justly?* Durham, N.C.: Duke University Press, 1961.

_____ , with Stanley Hauerwas. *Speak Up for Just War or Pacifism.* University Park, Pa.: Pennsylvania State University Press, 1988.

Russell, Frederick H. *The Just War in the Middle Ages.* Cambridge: Cambridge University Press, 1975.

Ryan, John A. and Boland, Francis J., CSC. *Catholic Principles of Politics.* New York: MacMillan, 1947.

Tucker, Robert. *The Just War.* Baltimore, Md.: Johns Hopkins University Press, 1960.

Walters, LeRoy Brandt. *Five Classic Just-War Theories: A Study in the Thought of Thomas Aquinas, Vitoria, Suarez, Gentili, and Grotius.* New Haven: Yale University Press, 1973.

Walzer, Michael. *Just and Unjust Wars.* New York: Basic Books, 1977 (2d ed., 1992).

Selective Bibliography on Nonviolent Defense Alternatives

American Friends Service Committee. *In Place of War: An Inquiry into Non-Violent National Defense.* New York: Grossman, 1962.

Atheston, Edward B. "The Relevance of Civilian-Based Defense to US Security Interests," *The Military Review* (May 1976), 24ff. (June 1976), 45ff.

Baez, Joan. "Personal Commitment to Nonviolent Social Change." In Israel W. Charny, ed. *Strategies Against Violence, Design for Nonviolent Change.* Boulder: Westview Press, 1978.

Boserup, Anders, and Andrew Mack. *War Without Weapons.* New York: Schocken, 1975.

Bruyn, Severyn. "Social Theory of Nonviolent Action: A Framework for Research in Creative Conflict." In Severyn T. Bruyn and Paula Rayman, eds. *Nonviolent Action and Social Change.* New York: Irvington Publishers, 1979.

Crowell, George H. *The Case for Nonviolent Civilian Defence against External Aggression.* Waterloo, Ont.: Ploughshares Working Paper 90-94, 1990.

Deutsch, Morton. *The Resolution of Conflict.* New Haven: Yale University Press, 1973.

Freund, Norman C. *Nonviolent National Defense.* New York: University Press of America, 1987.

Geeraerts, Gustaaf, ed. *Possibilities of Civilian Defense in Western Europe.* Amsterdam: Swets and Zeitlinger, 1977.

Gregg, Richard B. *The Power of Nonviolence.* Philadelphia: Lippincott, 1934.

Hare, A.P., and Herbert Blumberg, eds. *Nonviolent Direct Action: American Cases.* Washington, D.C.: Corpus, 1986.

_____ . *Liberation Without Violence.* Totowa, N.J.: Rowman and Littlefield, 1977.

Hughan, Jessie Wallace, and Hinshaw, Cecil. "Toward a Nonviolent National Defense." In Mulford Q. Sibley, ed. *The Quiet Battle.* Garden City, N.Y.: Doubleday, 1963; Chicago: Quadrangle, 1963; Boston: Beacon, 1968.

Irwin, Bob. *U.S. Defense Policy: Mainstream Views and Nonviolent Alternatives.* Waltham, Mass.: ISTNVA, 1982.

King-Hall, Stephen. *Defense in a Nuclear Age.* Nyack, N.Y.: Fellowship, 1959.

Lakey, George. "Sociological Mechanisms of Nonviolence." In Bruyn and Rayman, *Nonviolent Action and Social Change.*

Moulton, Phillips P. "Violence or Aggressive Nonviolent Resistance?" Wallingford, Penn.: Pendle Hill Pamphlet #178.

Norman, Liane Ellison. "Non-Violence Defined." In Ronald Stone and Dana Wilbanks, eds. *Peacemaking Struggle.* Lanham, Md.: University Press of America, 1985.

Roberts, Adam, ed. *The Strategy of Civilian Defense.* London: Faber & Faber, 1970; Baltimore: Penguin, 1969, under the title *Civilian Resistance and National Defense.*

Schell, Jonathan. "The Choice" (1982). In Donna Gregory, ed., *The Nuclear Predicament.* New York: St. Martin's Press, 1986.

Seifert, Harvey. *Conquest by Suffering.* Philadelphia: Westminster, 1965.

Sharp, Gene. *Exploring Nonviolent Alternatives.* Boston: Porter Sargent, 1970.

_____ . *Gandhi as a Political Strategist.* Boston: Porter Sargent, 1979.

_____ . *Making the Abolition of War a Realistic Goal.* New York: Institute for World Order, 1980.

_____ . *Making Europe Unconquerable: A Civilian Based Deterrence and Defense System.* London: Taylor/Francis, 1984; Cambridge: Bellinger, 1986.

_____ . *National Security Through Civilian-Based Defense.* Omaha: Association for Transarmament Studies, 1985.

_____ . *The Politics of Nonviolent Action,* 3 vols. Boston: Porter Sargent, 1973.

_____ . *Social Power and Political Freedom.* Boston: Porter Sargent, 1989.

Shridharani, Krishnalal Jethalal. *War Without Violence.* New York: Harcourt Brace, 1939.

Sider, Ronald, and Richard Taylor. *Nuclear Holocaust and Christian Hope.* Downers Grove: InterVarsity Press, 1982. See especially the chapter "International Aggression and Nonmilitary Defense," printed in *The Christian Century* 6/13 (July 1983), 643-47.

Smoke, Richard. *Paths to Peace.* Boulder: Westview Press, 1987.

Wehr, Paul. "Nonviolent Resistance to Occupation in Norway and Czechoslovakia." In Bruyn and Rayman, *Nonviolent Action and Social Change,* 213ff.

Periodicals

Nonviolent Sanctions: News from the Albert Einstein Institution. Albert Einstein Institution, 1430 Massachusetts Avenue, Cambridge, MA 02138.

Civilian-Based Defense: News and Opinion. Civilian-Based Defense Association, PO Box 31616, Omaha, NE 68131.

Further Writings by John Howard Yoder on the Just-War Tradition

"Bluff or Revenge: The Watershed in Democratic Deterrence Awareness." In Todd Whitmore, ed., *Ethics in the Nuclear Age*, Dallas: AMU Press, 1989, 79-92.

Christian Attitudes to War, Peace, and Revolution, a Companion to Bainton (non-trade book) (Elkhart, 1983), out of print. Duplicated copies available from Cokesbury Bookstore, Duke Divinity School, Durham N.C. See the following pages for the just-war tradition: 37-112, 455-86, 557-78.

"A Consistently Utilitarian Variant within the Just War Family." *Faith & Philosophy* 2/2 (April 1985), 112-19.

"The Constantinian Sources of Western Social Ethics." *The Priestly Kingdom.* Notre Dame, Ind.: University of Notre Dame Press, 1984, 135-47.

"The Credibility and Political Uses of the Just War Tradition." In George Lopez and Drew Christiansen, eds., *Morals and Might.* Boulder: Westview, 1995. Also available as Working Paper 1:C(ED):12 from the Joan B. Kroc Institute for International Peace Studies, Notre Dame, IN 46556.

"The Credibility of Ecclesiastical Teaching on the Morality of War." In Leroy S. Rouner, ed., *Celebrating Peace.* Notre Dame, Ind.: University of Notre Dame Press, 1990, 33-51.

"David Urquhart and the Challenge of 'Just War' at Vatican I." Working paper 3:WP:8, available from the Joan B. Kroc Institute for International Peace Studies, Notre Dame, IN 46556.

"How Many Ways Are There to Think about the Morality of War?" *Journal of Law and Religion* 11/1 (Summer 1995) , 83-107.

"Military Realities and Teaching the Laws of War." In Theodore Runyon, ed., *Theology, Politics, and Peace.* Maryknoll, N.Y.: Orbis Books, 1989, 176-80.

"The Moral Responsibility to Refuse to Serve in Unjust War." Working Paper 3:WP:9, available from the Joan B. Kroc Institute for International Peace Studies, Notre Dame, IN 46556.

"The Reception of the Just War Tradition by the Magisterial Reformation." *History of European Ideas* 9/1 (1986): 1-23.

"Religious Perspectives on the Use of Force." Conference paper for the United States Institute of Peace (April 1992). Working Paper 3:WP:10, available from the Joan B. Kroc Institute for International Peace Studies, Notre Dame, IN 46556.

"Surrender: A Moral Imperative." *Review of Politics* 48/4 (Fall 1986): 576-95.